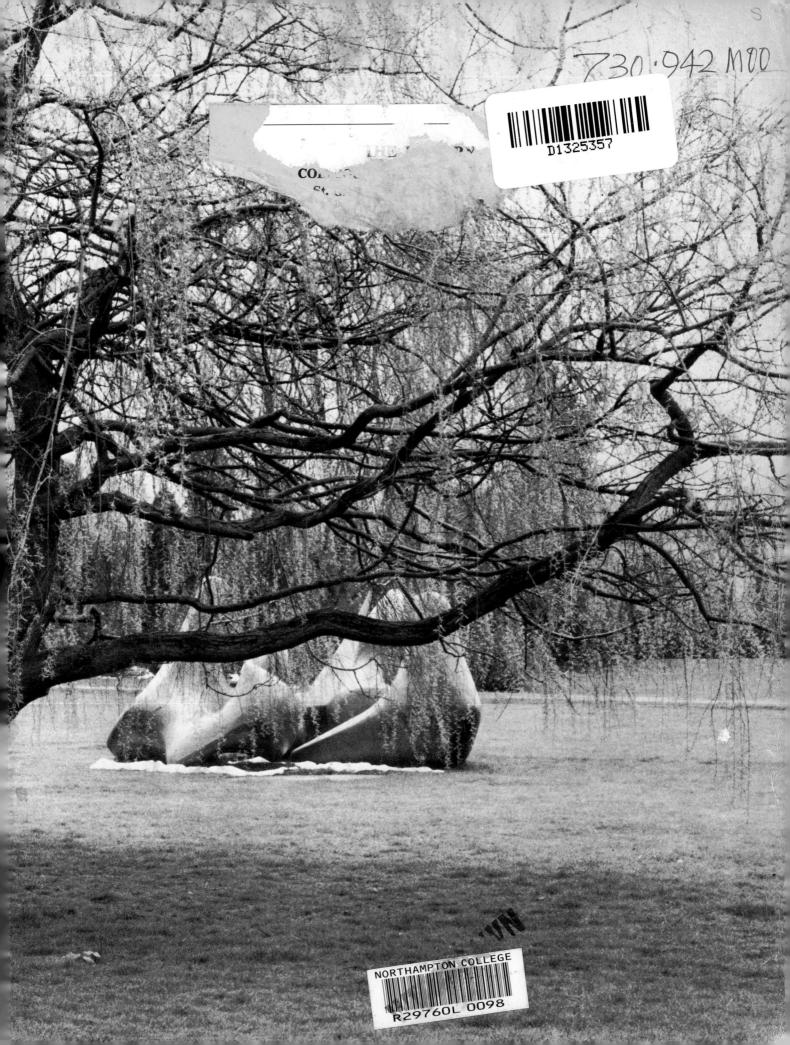

The avenue through the coppice, looking past *Seated Man* 1949, in cast concrete

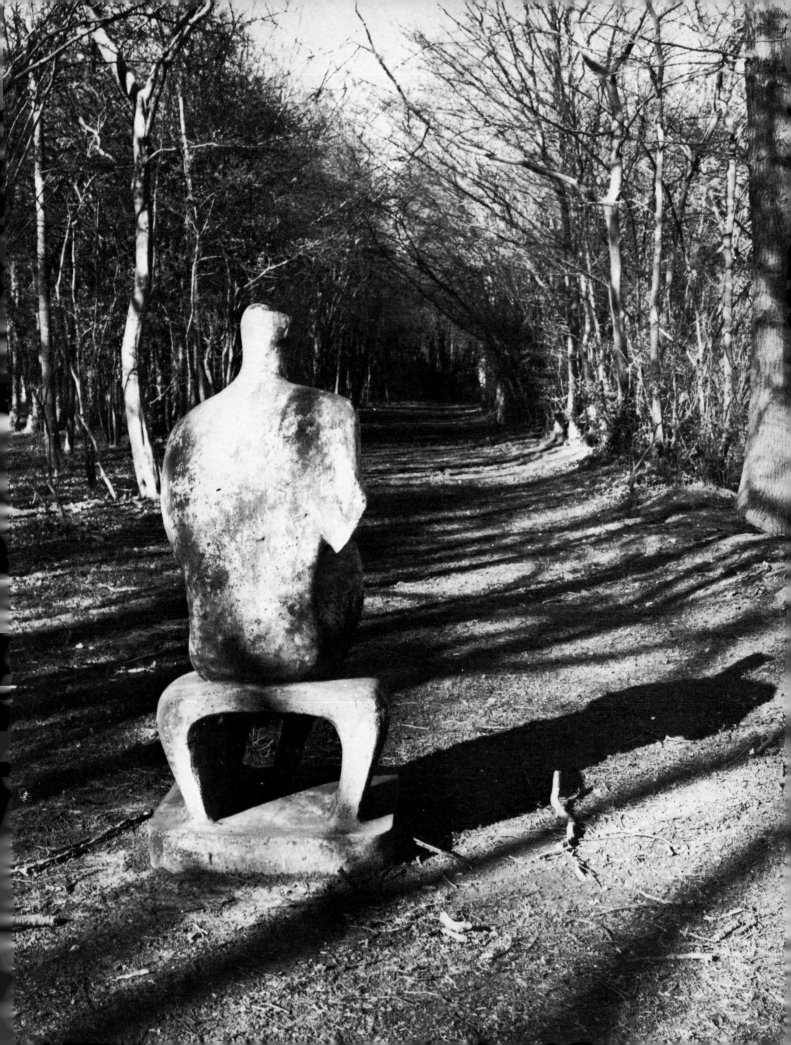

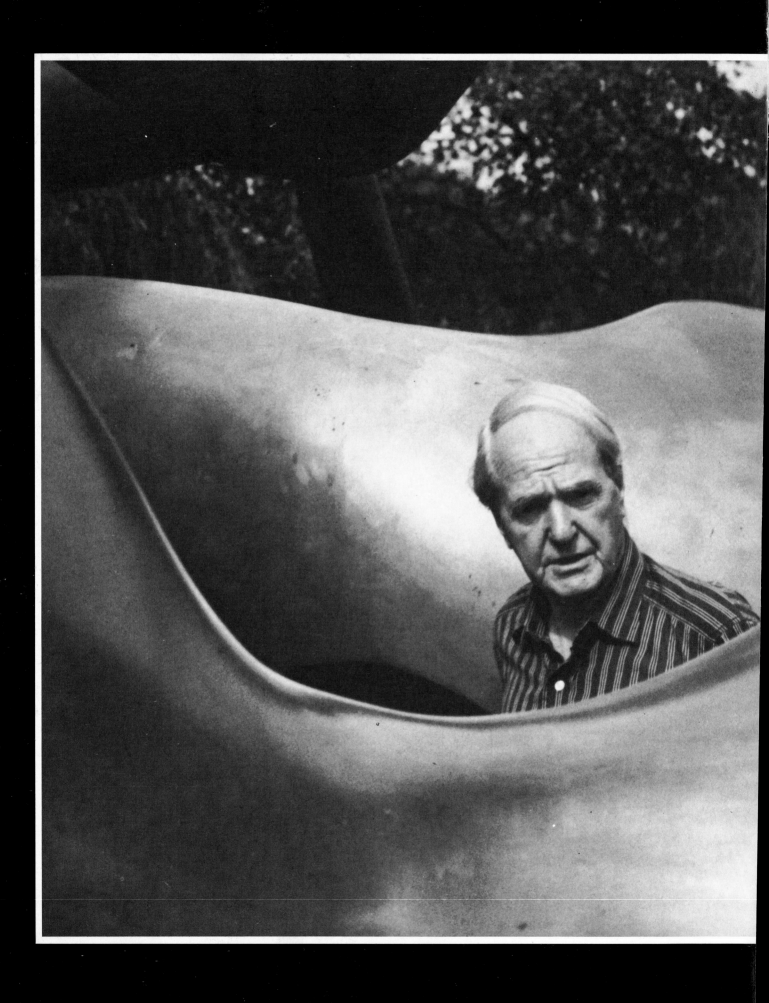

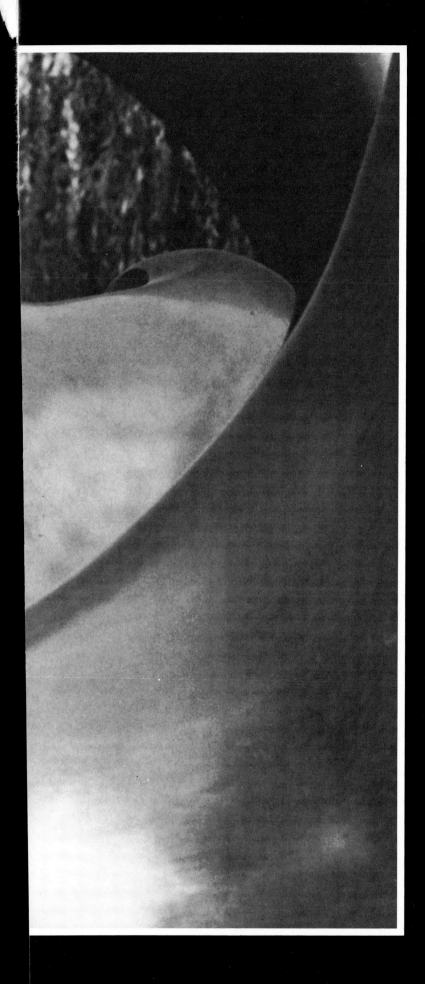

With
HENRY
MOORE

The Artist at Work
Photographed by
Gemma Levine

Sidgwick & Jackson
London

Acknowledgments

I should like to thank the following for their help and work in the preparation of this book: David Mitchinson, Henry Moore's archivist, for his invaluable guidance; Margaret Willes, my editor at Sidgwick and Jackson; Paul Watkins, the designer; Mrs Betty Tinsley, Henry Moore's secretary; Gordon Bishop Associates Ltd; and Olympus Cameras.

Gemma Levine July 1978

Front and rear endpapers: Mrs Moore walking through the grounds at Hoglands, between *Oval with Points* 1968/70, in bronze, and the units of *Three Piece Sculpture: Vertebrae* 1968/9

First published in Great Britain in 1978 by
Sidgwick & Jackson
Text copyright © 1978 Henry Moore
Photographs copyright © 1978 Gemma Levine
Preface copyright © 1978 David Mitchinson

ISBN 0 283 984600

Design by Paul Watkins

Colour origination by
Newsele Litho Limited, 25-20142 Milano, Italy
Printed & bound in Great Britain by
W. S. Cowell Ltd., Butter Market, Ipswich
for Sidgwick & Jackson Ltd
1 Tavistock Chambers
Bloomsbury Way
London WC1A 2SG

Contents

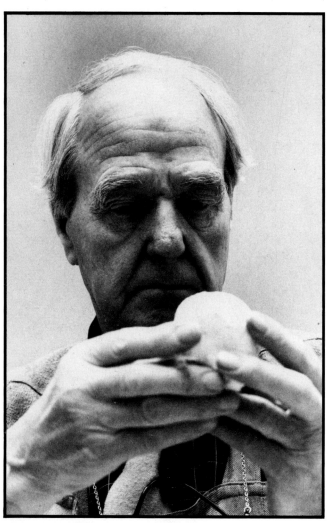

Preface by David Mitchinson

There can be very few among us who, on reaching our eightieth birthday, are still able to have our daily routine 'at work' recorded photographically. Henry Moore at eighty is undoubtedly the greatest sculptor of our age and one of the most esteemed figures in our national life. Success did not come early to him. It is only since the end of the last war, when he was already in his late forties, that the public generally became aware of his work. He is a home-loving, family man, still maintaining a simple, unspoilt life style despite the many honours and distinctions granted to him over the last three decades. His daily routine remains much the same as it has always been.

Breakfast is at 8.00 a.m., work begins in the office at 9.30 with Moore hurrying away to the studios by 10.00 if possible, back for a hot drink at 11.00 and then more work until lunch at 1.00 p.m. Lunch is the main meal of the day, and his wife Irina, who is a strict timekeeper, allows no one to break her 'lunch at one' rule. He has a short rest after the meal and is back to work again at 2.30. Some afternoons are interrupted by visitors and everything stops for tea at 4.00. After tea, there may perhaps follow a period of letter answering, something Moore dislikes spending time on, preferring to use the telephone whenever he can. By 6.30, the staff have left, and he then goes down to the graphic studio for another hour's work before supper. Naturally, this routine is broken – visits abroad to look at sculpture sites or to check on exhibitions, visits to London, to museums, galleries or printers, all disturb work in the studio, but these visits are now kept to an absolute minimum.

In any creative activity, there has to be the closest co-operation between the artist and those assistants and craftsmen who work with him. Designers, printers, exhibition planners, architects, foundrymen, builders, and many other groups of specialists have their parts to play before the artist's work can be seen and appreciated by the general public. Among these groups are photographers. Here I would like to thank Gemma Levine for the creative and informative treatment of her subject.

There are many books on Henry Moore but this is the first occasion that an intimate book, showing the man in his own surroundings and at his everyday tasks, has been attempted.

Mrs Levine was only allowed to begin photography on the understanding that she remained in the background and did not interrupt the artist while he was working. She spent some time in 1976 and 1977 visiting the studios and looking over the grounds, taking the occasional photograph, before she started to be a frequent visitor in December 1977. For the next five months, she was about whenever it was possible or practical, preparing for this publication. Since the deadline on pictures needed for this book, she has continued taking photographs of Moore's work in general, and is now a familiar figure on the Much Hadham scene.

Most of her photographs have been taken in and around the Moores' home, Hoglands, at Much Hadham in Hertfordshire. For those not familiar with the topography of the Hoglands estate, I should explain that it consists of many acres of garden, park and farm land, bought over the last thirty years. On this are spaced nine different studios.

The house dates mainly from the seventeenth century, was originally two cottages and has only recently been made one on the upper storey. The Moores built on some extensions at the back of the house in the early 1960s. The front faces Perry Green, a hamlet one mile from Much Hadham. Immediately adjacent to the house is Henry Moore's original studio, now called the 'House' or 'Top' Studio, and used mainly for finishing and photographing small or medium-sized sculptures. Directly behind it is a little room used in the last eight years for etching. Prior to this, it was the original maquette studio. Beyond the gardens of Hoglands, at the back of the house, are the 'Meccano' or 'Plastic' Studio, constructed in 1963, the new maquette studio, built in 1970 when the original maquette studio was taken over for etching, the White Studio with its loading bay, and

the carving studio. Behind these is the Sheep Barn with the grounds stretching away towards the sheep fields, hill, coppice and small lake.

On the left of Hoglands is the garden of Gildmore House, with its maquette and graphic studios; the maquette studio was built three years ago, and the graphic studio was reconstructed in the previous year. On the right lies Dane Tree House, the newly opened headquarters of the Henry Moore Foundation. To this building is attached a new carving gallery. To save members of the family and the Henry Moore Foundation from intrusion, I should add that the studios and grounds are not open to the public.

Occasionally the camera left Hoglands and followed Henry Moore to the lithographic printers, the bronze foundry and to an outdoor exhibition to see finished works of art *in situ.*

The photographs in this book have been arranged quite informally into eight sections. The first two could be described as 'background': these are *Portraits of the Artist* and *Environment.* The next five all deal with some aspect of the artist at work: *Origin of Ideas* looks at the sources of inspiration; *Inside the Studio* examines what goes on in the work areas and to what uses they are put; *Progression of Ideas* takes two subjects (one sculpture, one graphic) and follows them through to completion; *Tools* looks at many of the things needed in the studio, some of them quite unexpected; and *Execution of Work* shows the artist himself working. The book ends logically with a section of *Finished Works.*

Although this is primarily a photographic book, arranged to tell a story, Henry Moore kindly consented to comment on the photographs and to enrich the pages with observations relating to the various subjects.

At the time that most of these photographs were being taken, Moore was working on a number of important projects, including the *Mirror Knife Edge,* the largest sculpture he has ever had cast in bronze, now in Washington D.C.

11

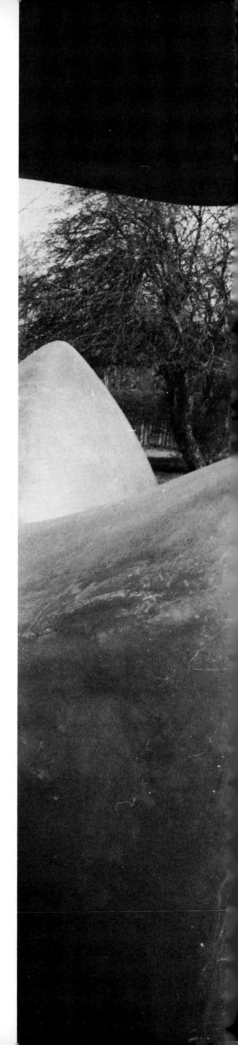

Gemma Levine photographed this sculpture during construction. She has also followed the progress of a new carving in elmwood called *Reclining Figure: Holes,* the first wood carving Moore has made for more than ten years.

Besides sculpture, Moore was busy on some new graphic projects – coloured etchings and aquatints for a new album of reclining figures and a group of individual lithographs, all of figures with architectural backgrounds. The book also includes photographs of many items from Moore's collection of natural forms and found-objects – bones, shells, flints, pieces of wood which have been inspirational for some of his sculpture.

One way for all of us to gain a greater understanding of the work of Henry Moore is to see more clearly the man; that is what this book has set out to portray. In conclusion, I would like to repeat my thanks to Gemma Levine and to Henry Moore for their collaboration and working relationship, without which which this publication would not have been possible.

David Mitchinson
Blackheath July 1978

Henry Moore rearranging units of *Three Piece Sculpture: Vertebrae* 1968/9, in the grounds of Hoglands

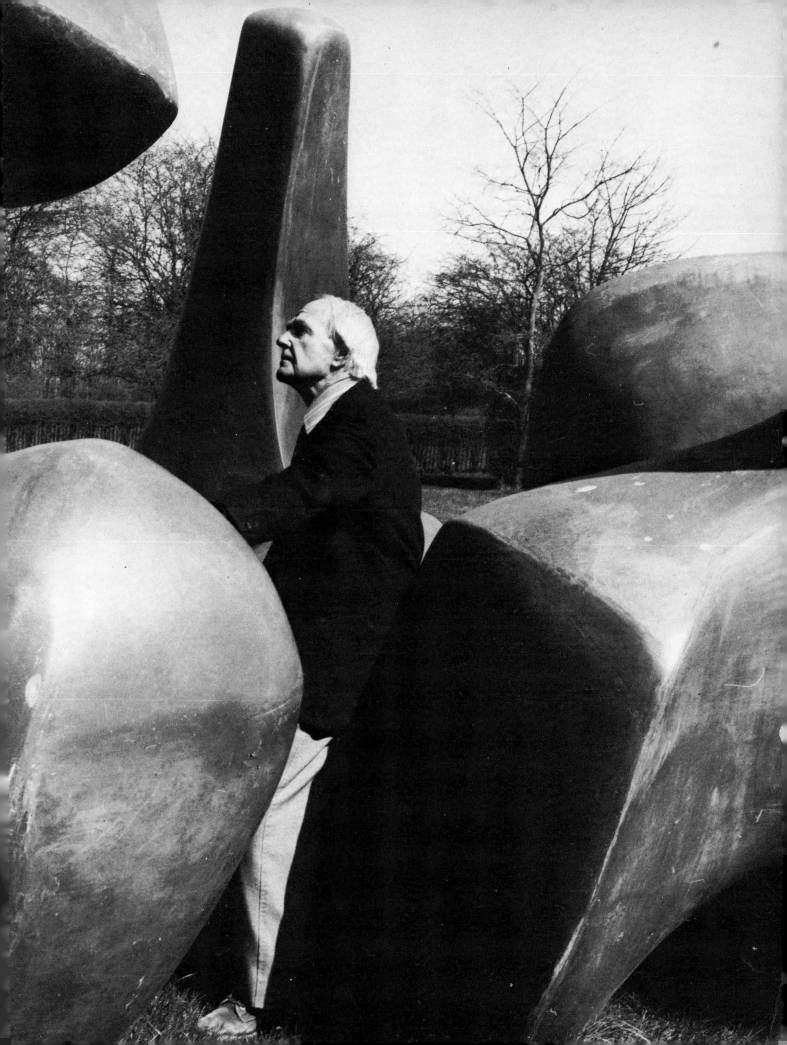

Portraits of the Artist

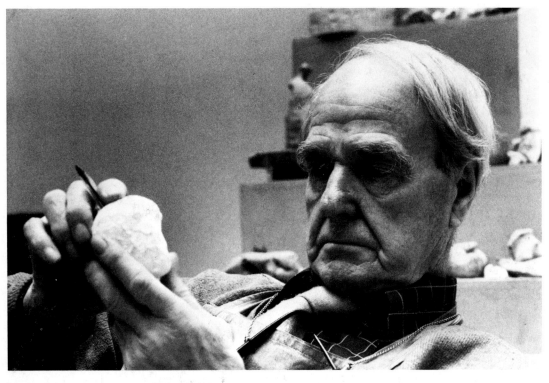

Henry Moore studying a small plaster head

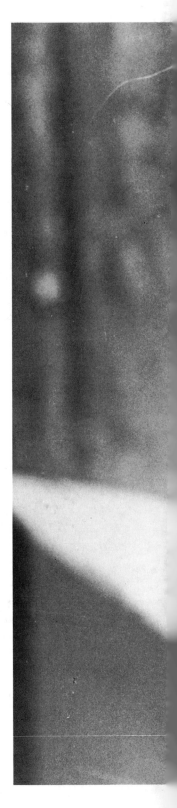

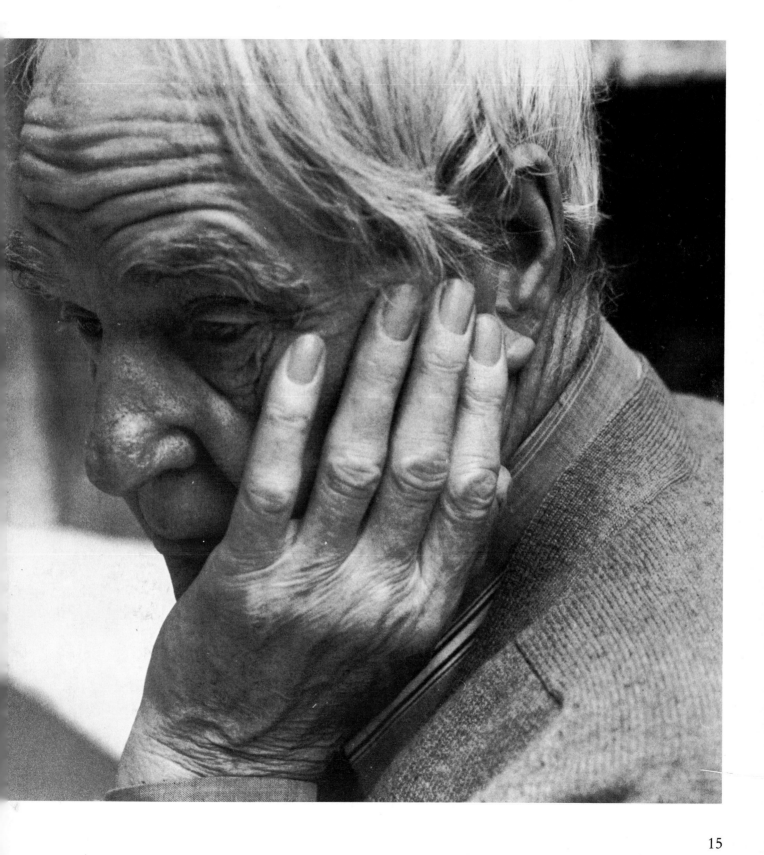

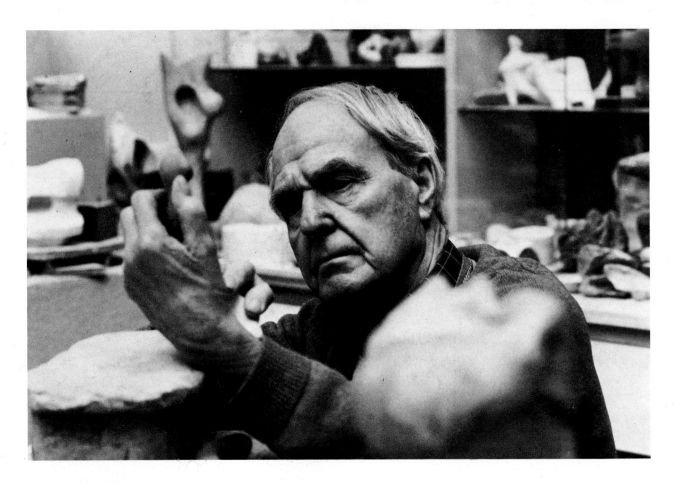

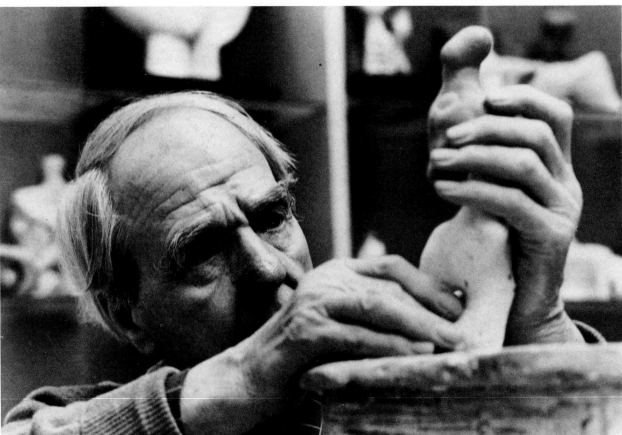

The sculptor studying different found-objects in his maquette studio

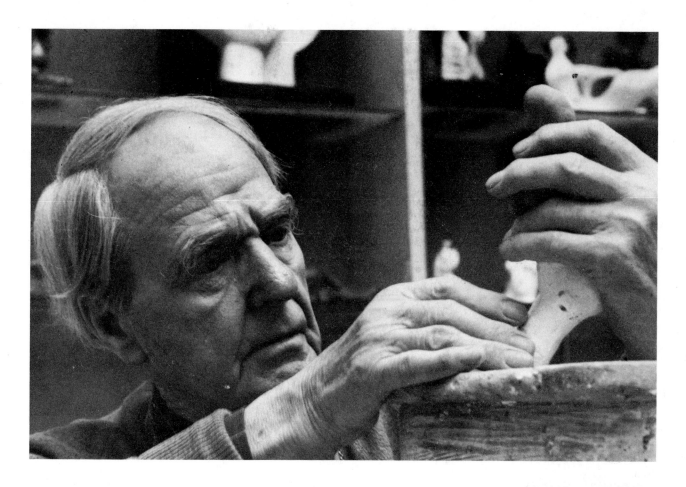

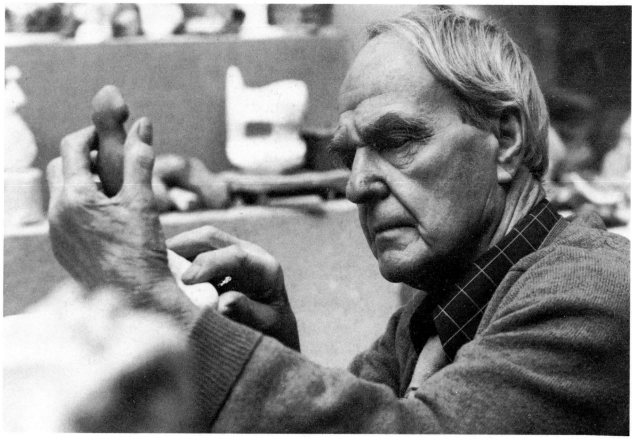

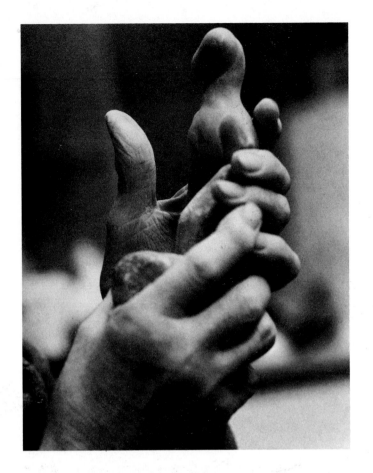
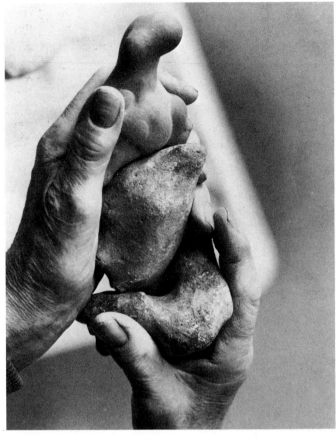
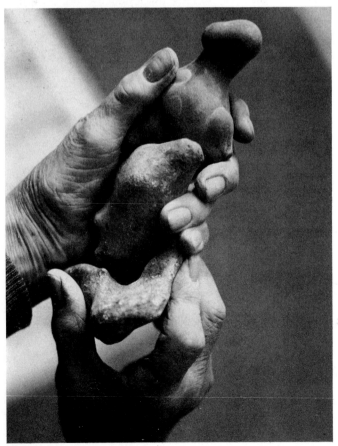
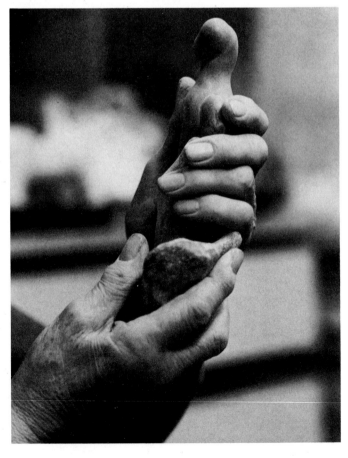

The hands of the sculptor

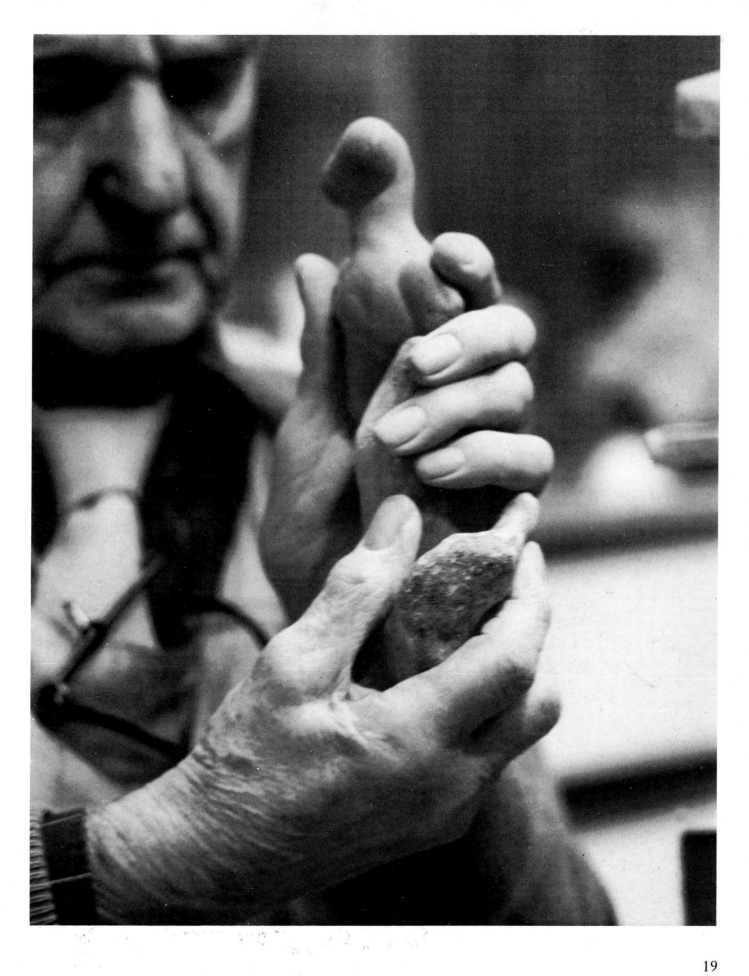

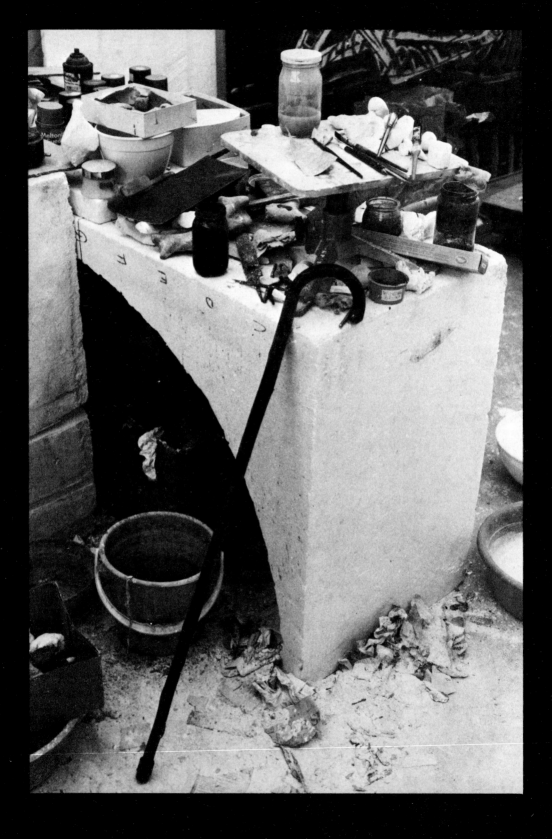

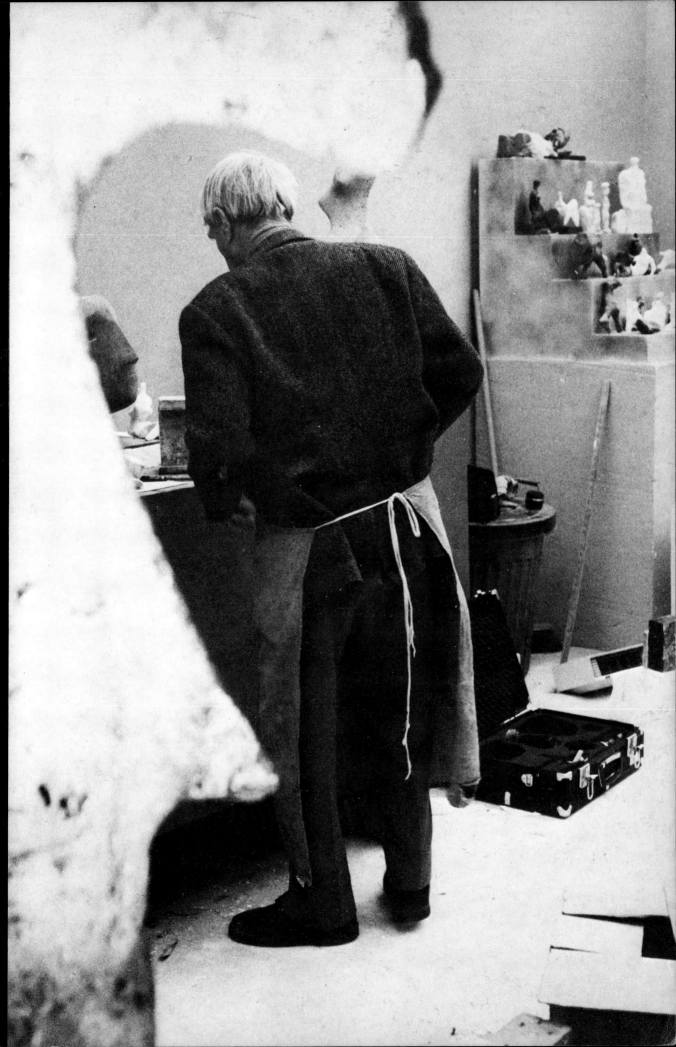

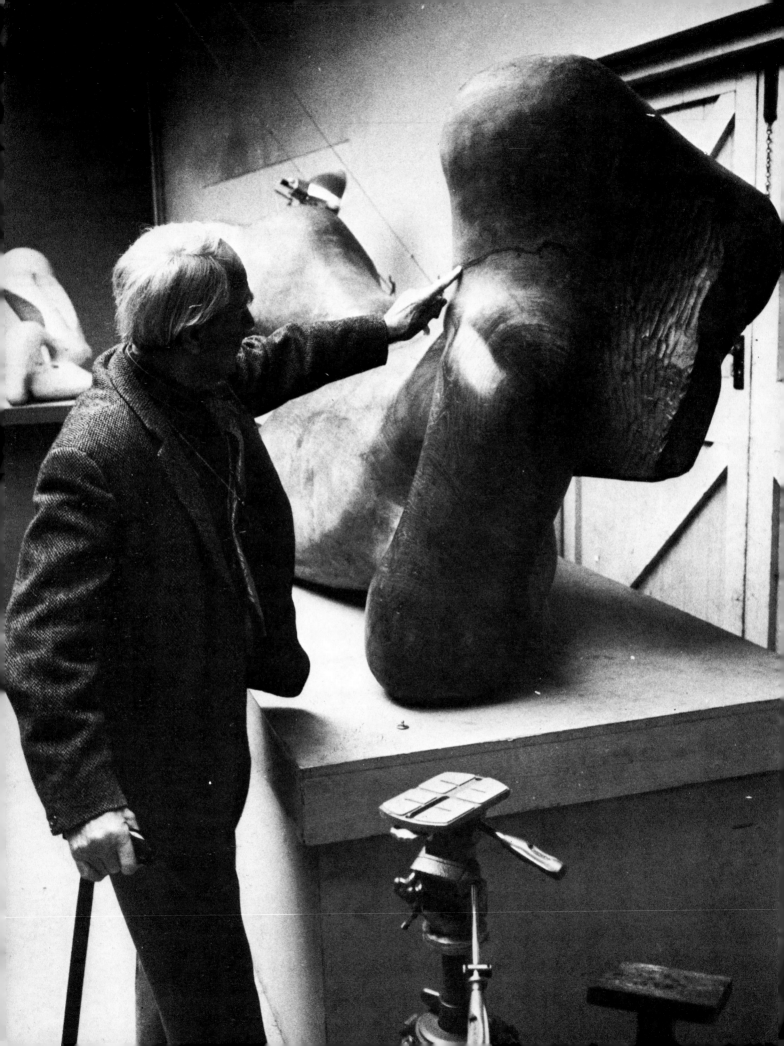

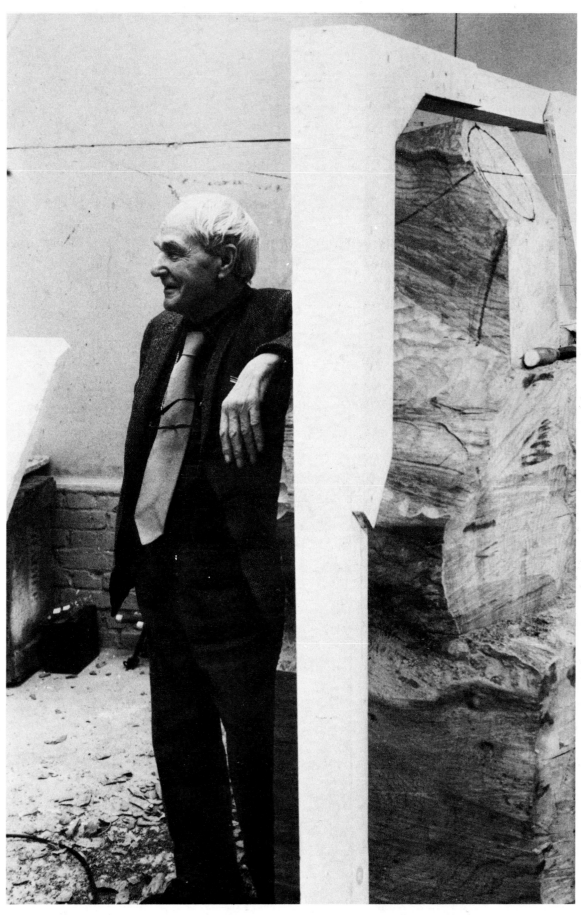

Henry Moore in the carving studio at an early stage of *Reclining Figure* 1976/8, in elmwood
Left: Henry Moore pointing to a small split appearing in the wood of *Reclining Figure* 1959/64, elmwood

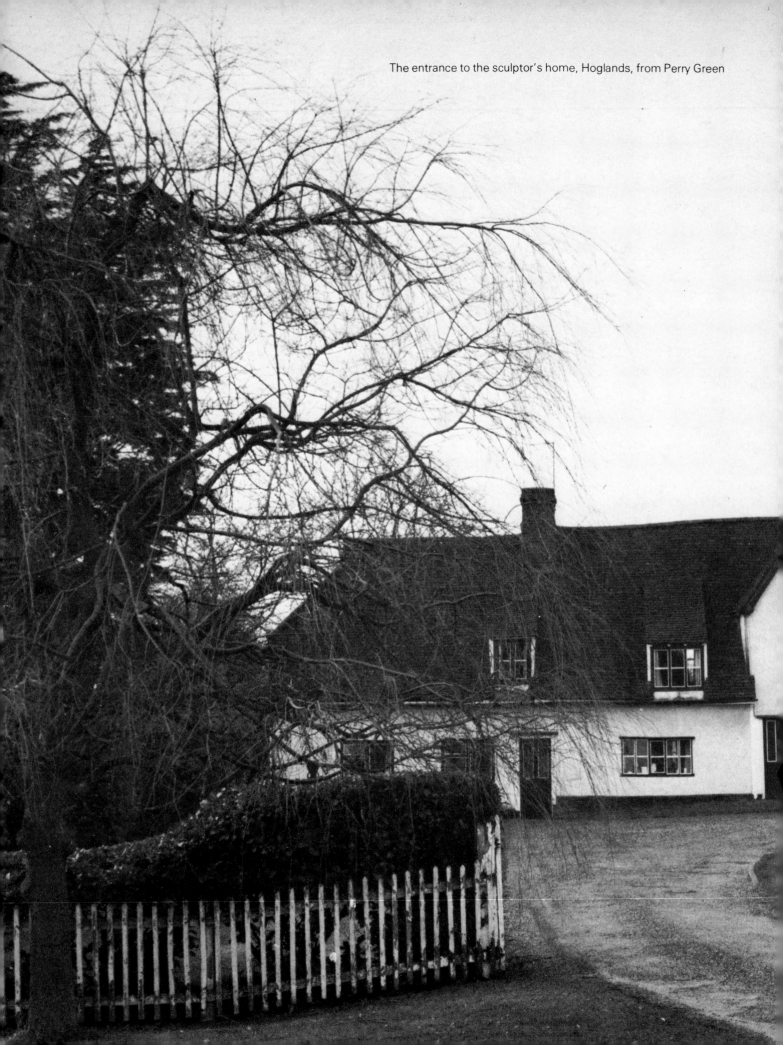

The entrance to the sculptor's home, Hoglands, from Perry Green

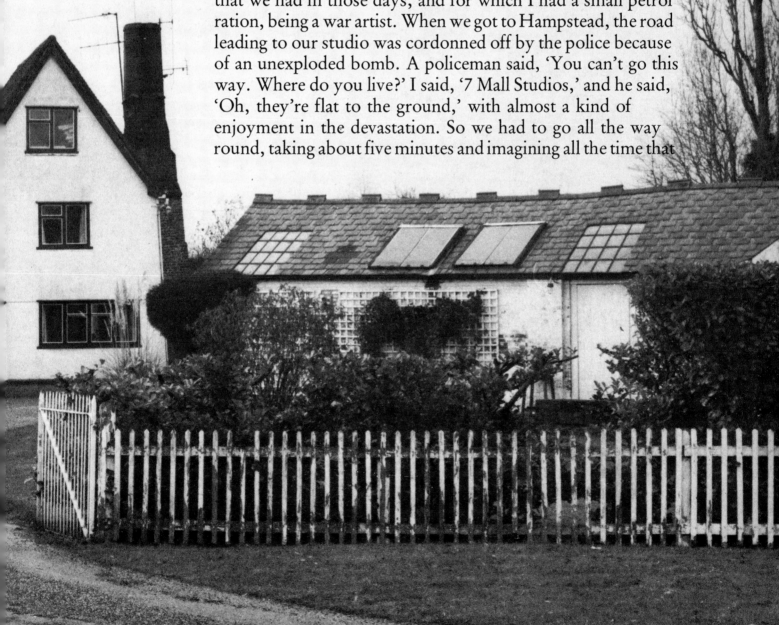

Environment

We came here in 1941, when my studio in London was made unusable by a bomb falling nearby and it happened that we were not in London that weekend. We were staying in Much Hadham with friends only two or three hundred yards across from here in a little park called South End. We could see that there was a raid going on because it is near enough to London as the crow flies – only about twenty miles. The friends we had been staying with tried to persuade us to stay a little longer, but I said I was doing the Shelter Drawings and had to get back. We left them on the Monday morning in the little Standard Coupé that we had in those days, and for which I had a small petrol ration, being a war artist. When we got to Hampstead, the road leading to our studio was cordonned off by the police because of an unexploded bomb. A policeman said, 'You can't go this way. Where do you live?' I said, '7 Mall Studios,' and he said, 'Oh, they're flat to the ground,' with almost a kind of enjoyment in the devastation. So we had to go all the way round, taking about five minutes and imagining all the time that our studio was flat to the ground. However, he had mistaken it and it was Park Hill Studios that had the direct hit, but it was near enough our studio for it to be made unusable, with the windows and doors blown in. In those days you couldn't possibly get a house repaired within six or seven months but we had to have somewhere to live. I rang our Much Hadham weekend friend and said, 'We would like to come back as you were suggesting.'

Within a week we had found that half this house, Hoglands, was available to rent. It was near enough to London for me to travel backwards and forwards, spending the night in the shelters and coming back here the next day to do the drawings. You couldn't sit in the shelters and draw people undressing their children – it was too private.

In 1941, the house was in a very bad state, tumble-down and so on. Later we got the whole house. The owner wanted to sell, we bought it, and we have been here ever since, gradually making repairs. Ten or fifteen years ago, we built an extra room because there was no room facing the south that got the sunshine, and we acquired two extra areas of garden. Gradually it increased to several acres, so I could continue working out-of-doors.

We had always had a little cottage in the country – the first one in Kent cost us £87. So, on summer holidays away from teaching, I was always doing sculptures in the country. Finding Hoglands and its surrounding ground meant that I could continue my ambition to make sculptures which were intended to be seen principally in the open air. It has meant me developing my liking both for working in the open air and for having my sculptures seen in the open air. By the time the idea of the Battersea Park Exhibition came on the scene, I had already been working here for nearly ten years and I had done a lot of sculptures out-of-doors. There is my group of standing women in Battersea Park, which was first shown in that open air exhibition. I was the sculptor mainly responsible for placing and siting all the works in the exhibition – that is why I gave the best place to my own sculpture!

View from inside the house, looking south past
Working Model for Sundial 1965, in bronze

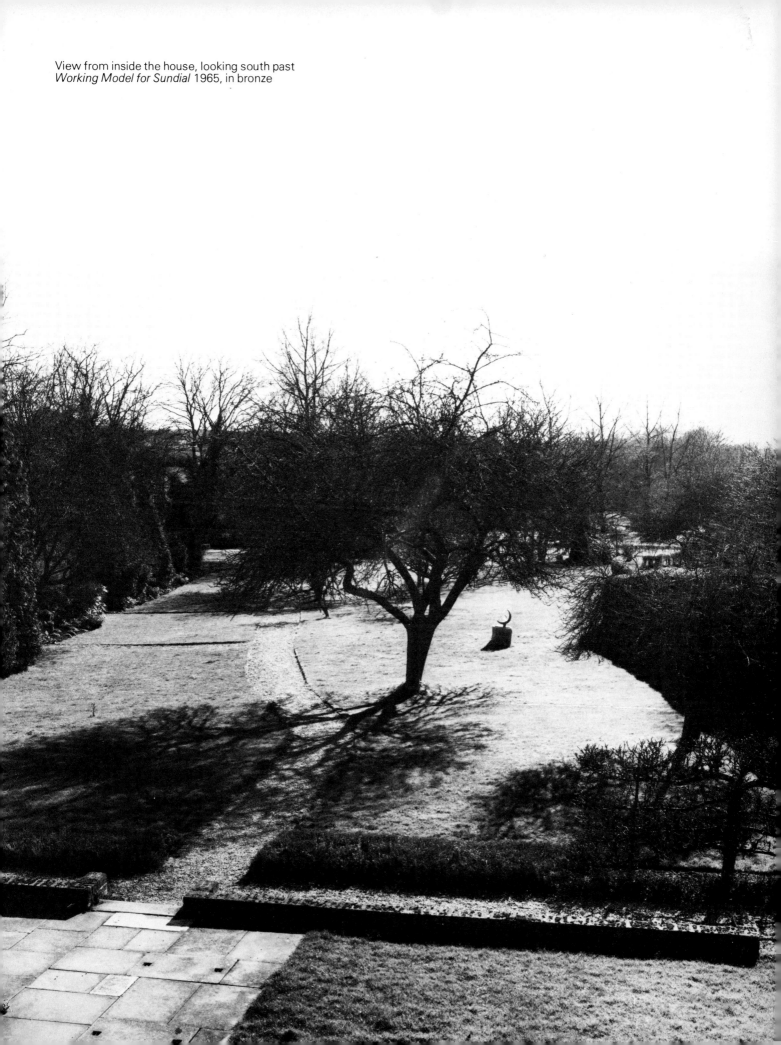

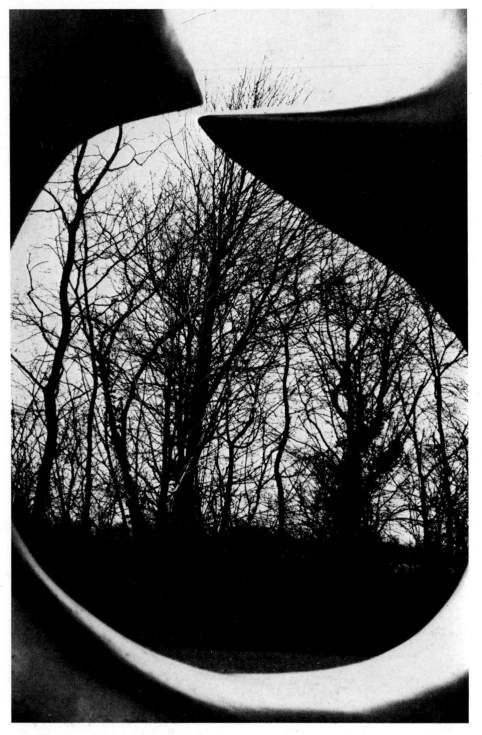

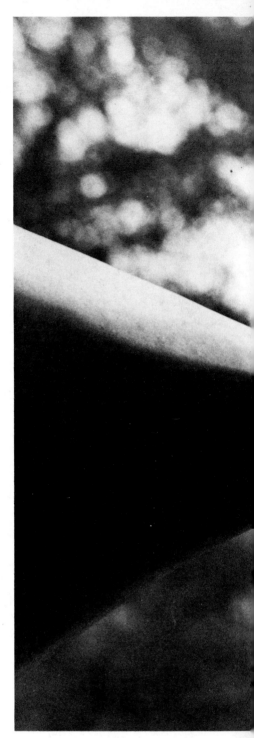

Details of *Oval with Points*

In 1940 I made a sculpture with three points, because this pointing has an emotional or physical action in it where things are just about to touch but don't. There is some anticipation of this action. Michaelangelo used the same theme in his fresco on the ceiling of the Sistine Chapel, of God creating Adam, in which the forefinger of God's hand is just about to touch and give life to Adam. It is also like the points in the sparking plug of a car, where the spark has to jump across the gap between the points.

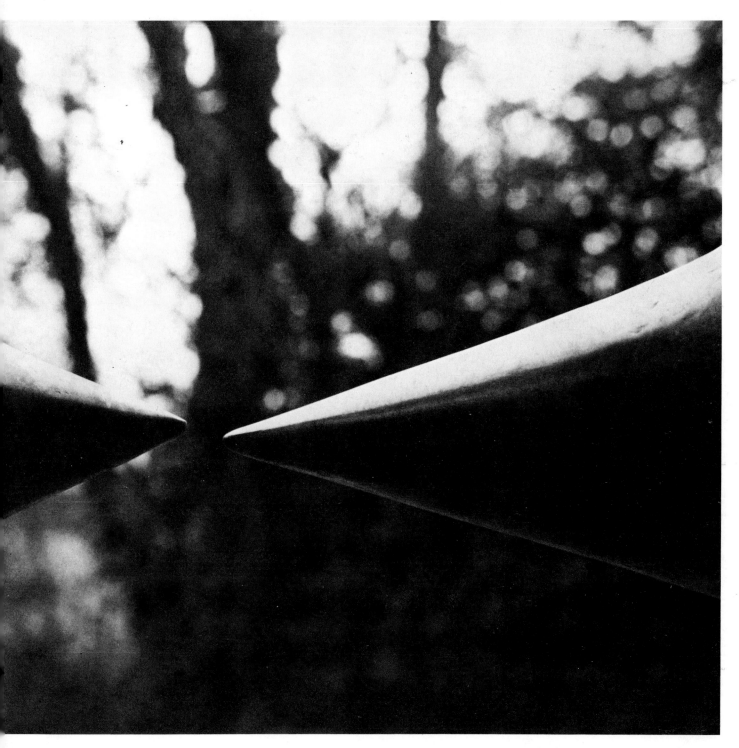

There is a very beautiful early French painting *(Gabrielle d'Estrées with her sister in the bath)*, where one sister is just about to touch the nipple of the other. I used this sense of anticipation first in the *Three Points* of 1940, but there are other, later works where one form is nearly making contact with the other. It is very important that the points do not actually touch. There has to be a gap.

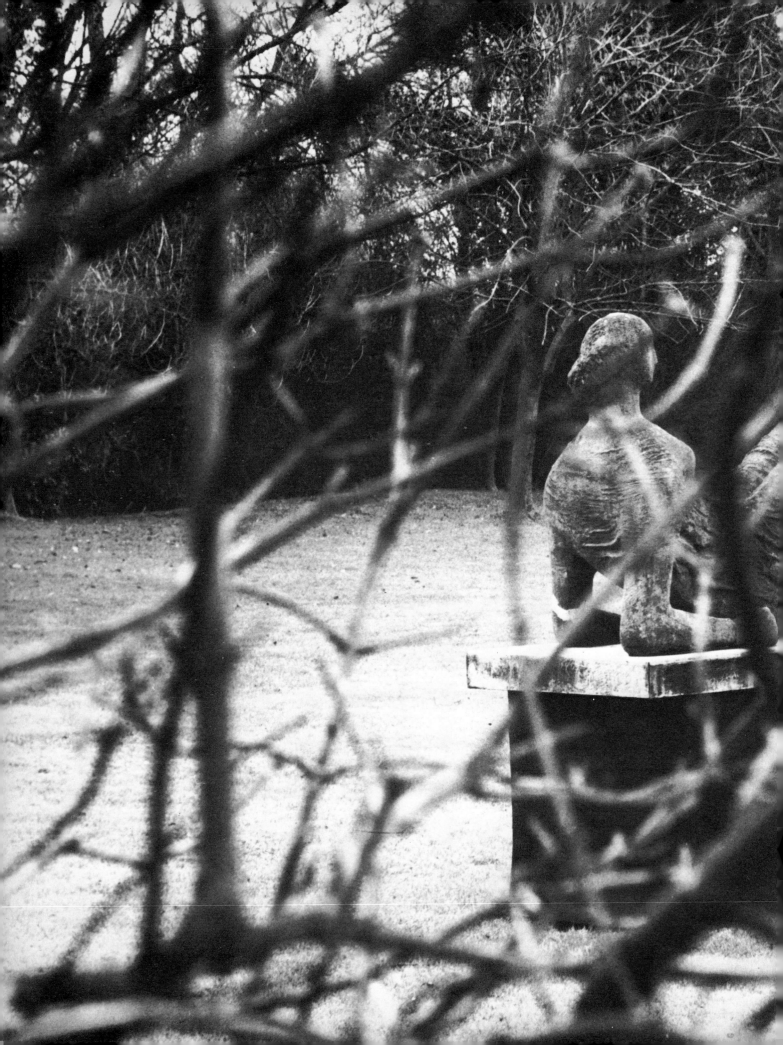

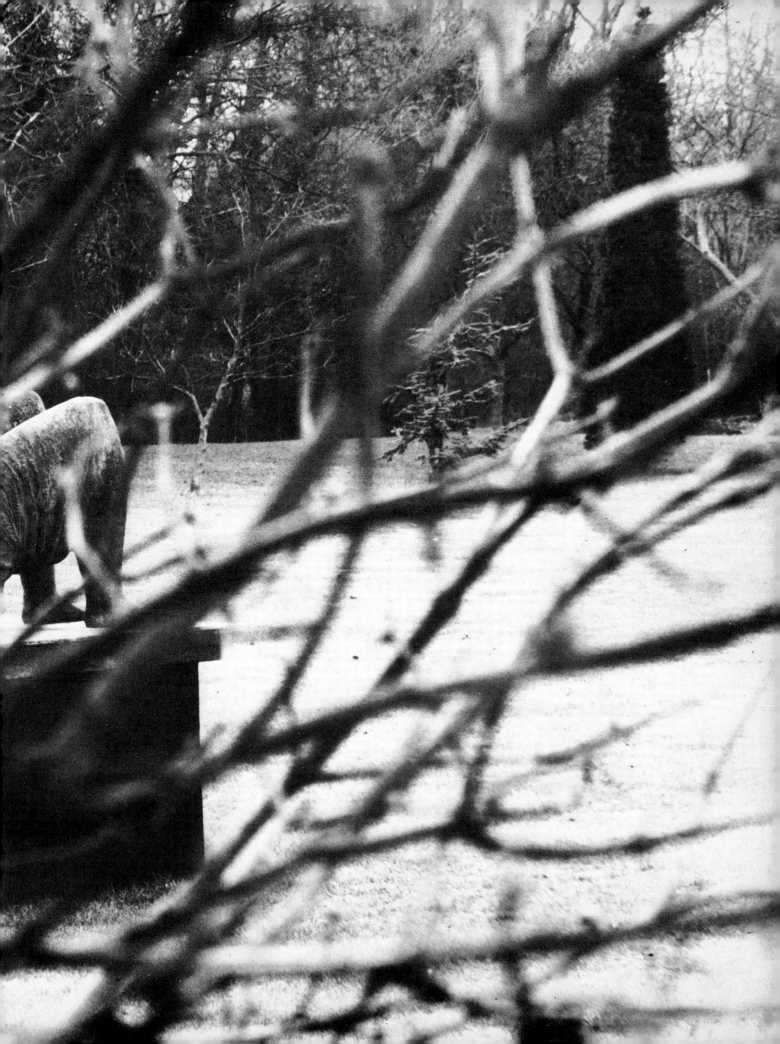

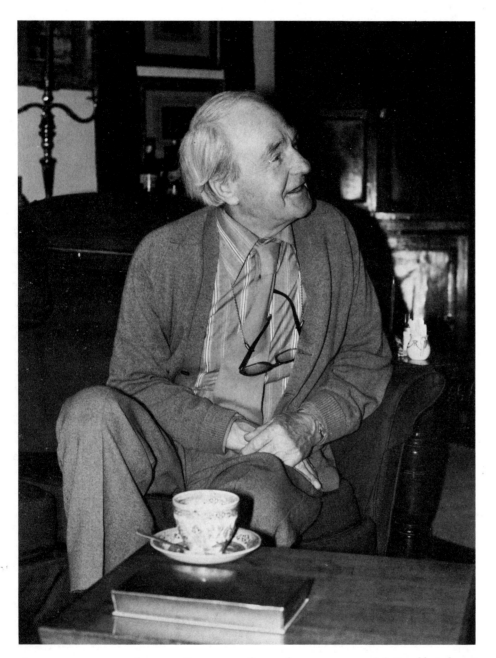

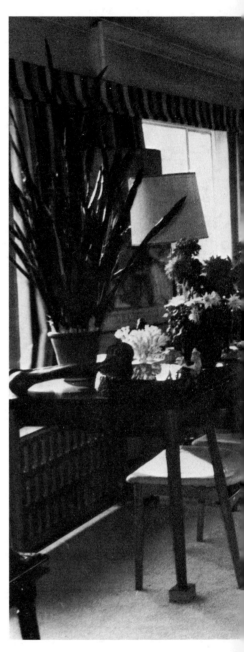

As a young sculptor, I never thought, nor could I afford, to have any work other than my own around me. It was enough that the British Museum and the National Gallery were there, and that I could go and look at their masterpieces. It is only gradually that I have acquired works of art, and I love having them around me now.

Left: Henry Moore enjoying an 11 a.m. break

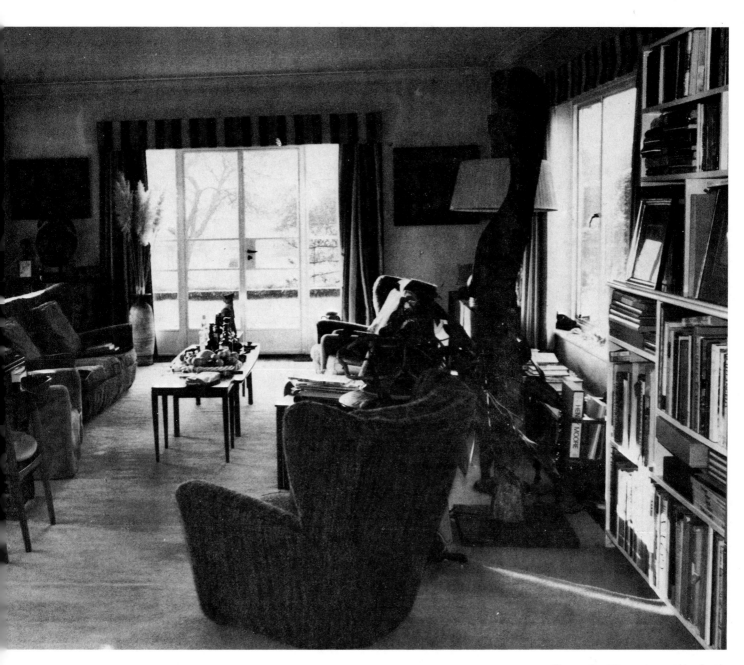

The main sitting-room at Hoglands

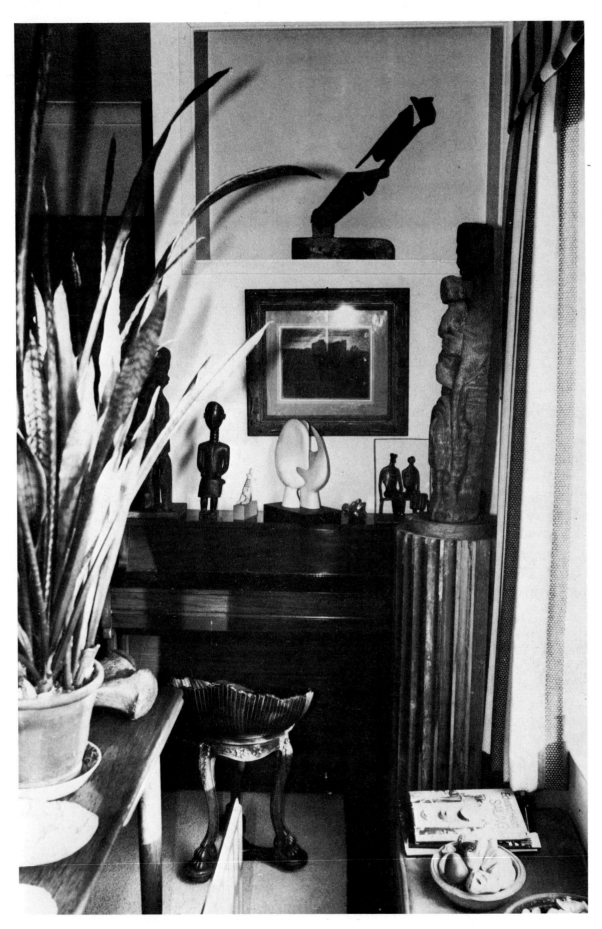

A corner of the sitting-room, showing some of the sculptor's
private collection of works of art and three of his maquettes

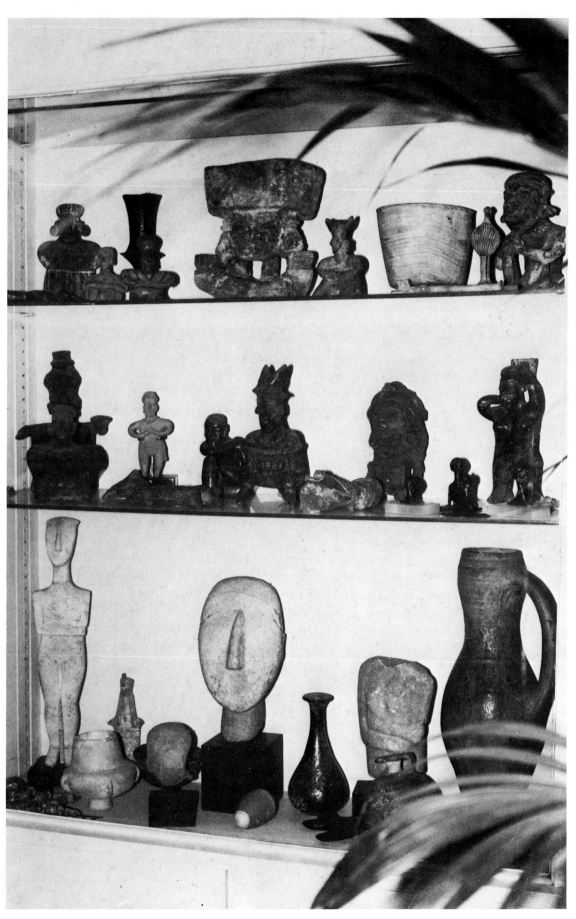

Vitrine with part of Henry Moore's collection,
including Pre-Columbian and Mexican figures

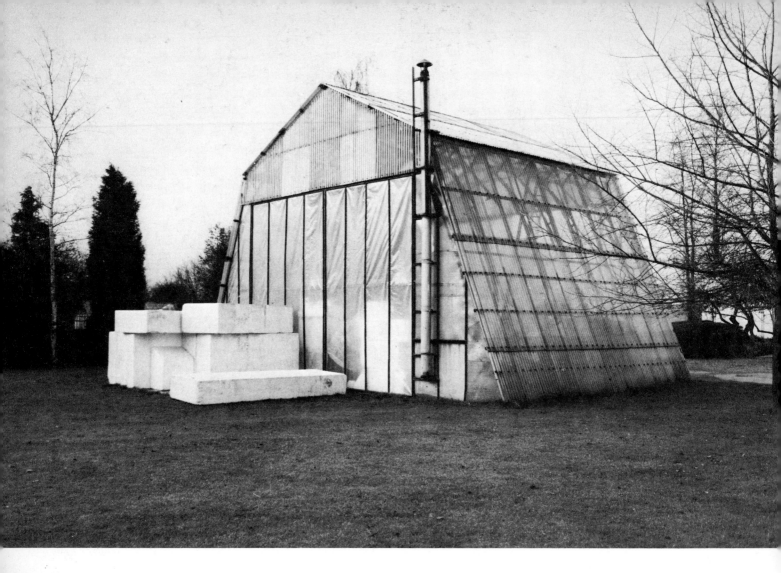

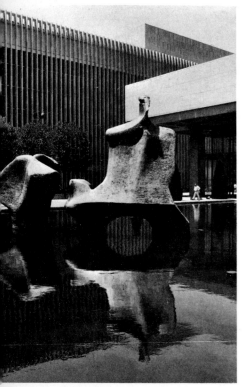

This studio dates from when I was asked to do a sculpture for the Lincoln Centre in New York about fifteen years ago. I knew the site was going to need a larger work than any I had done before – even larger than the UNESCO *Reclining Figure*. I knew that it was going to take me more than the summer to do it, and that I would have to work through the winter. Yet I realised that a big sculpture intended to live out-of-doors permanently is better if actually made out-of-doors. Light out-of-doors comes of course from the sky, it is an all-round light, it is not the directional light which you get in a room with windows. So I built this studio large enough for the Lincoln Centre sculpture, and yet so that I could use it as though it was out-of-doors. The construction is something like a Meccano Set, covered with transparent plastic material allowing the light to be virtually identical with outside, even in winter. In summer, when it is too hot, the sides can be taken out. Since 1963, this studio has been a tremendous asset to me. All my large sculptures have been made in this studio.

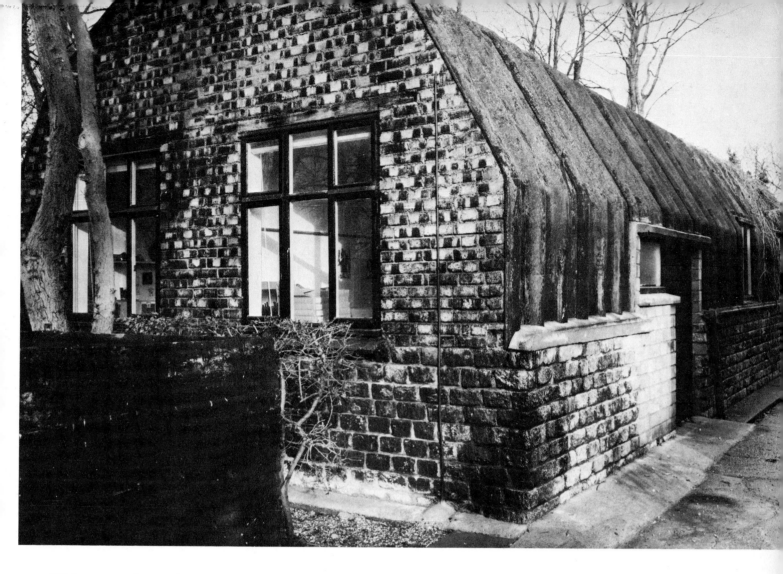

This was where the previous owner of next door did his book binding and gilding, which is why the property is called Gildmore. I turned the workshop where he did his gilding into this graphic studio.

Opposite: The Plastic Studio in winter with (below) *Reclining Figure* 1963/5, in bronze, outside the Lincoln Center for the Performing Arts, in New York

Above: The Gildmore graphic studio

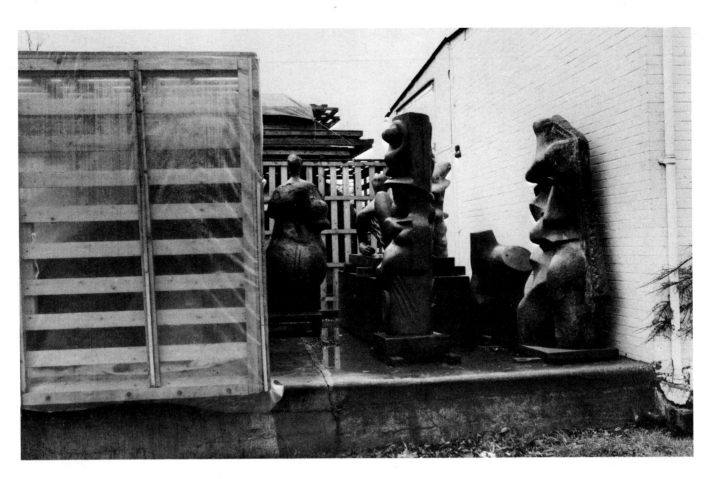

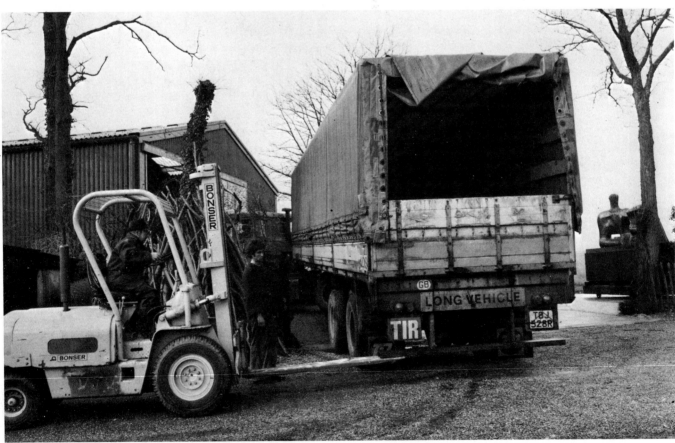

Left above: Loading bay outside the White Studio, with various works in bronze waiting for dispatch

Left below: Frank Farnham, Henry Moore's builder, with the forklift, preparing to load a lorry with sculpture for transportation to West Berlin

Below: John Farnham cleaning a bronze cast of *Three Piece Reclining Figure: Draped* 1975, in the sheep field

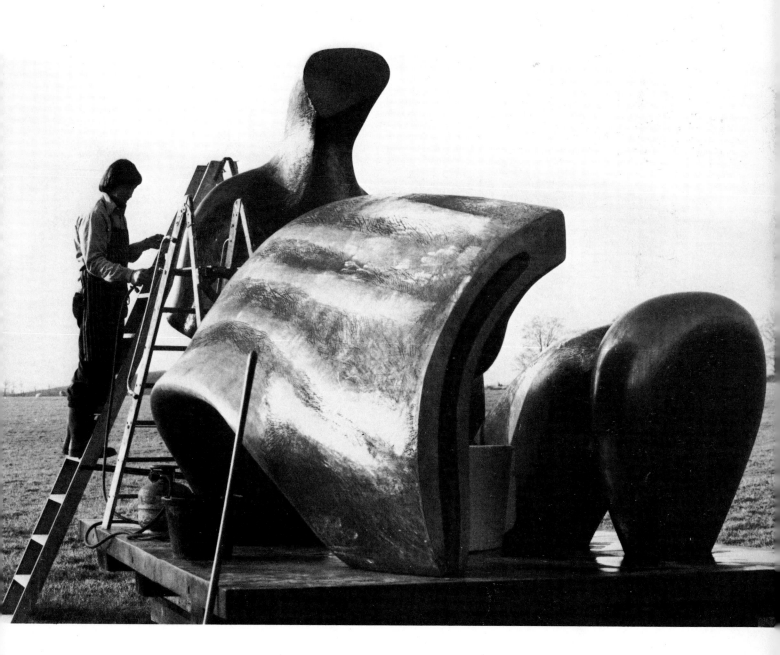

39

This small hill on the horizon is man-made. When I acquired the ground it was a pyramid of waste gravel. But you cannot put a sculpture on a pyramid if the point is too small, so I had a bulldozer and shaped it into a small hill (sometimes mistaken for a pre-historic barrow). Now I want to put a sculpture there. The sky is the perfect background for sculpture, because you are contrasting solid, three-dimensional form – the sculpture – with its opposite, the sky, which is space, with no distractions. A cast of *Three Piece Reclining Figure: Draped* will be tried out on the hill. This hill is first seen from three or four hundred yards away, and therefore a sculpture there needs to be of some size. The first things I tried on the hill were too small – from a distance they just looked as though there could be a stray sheep that had got there.

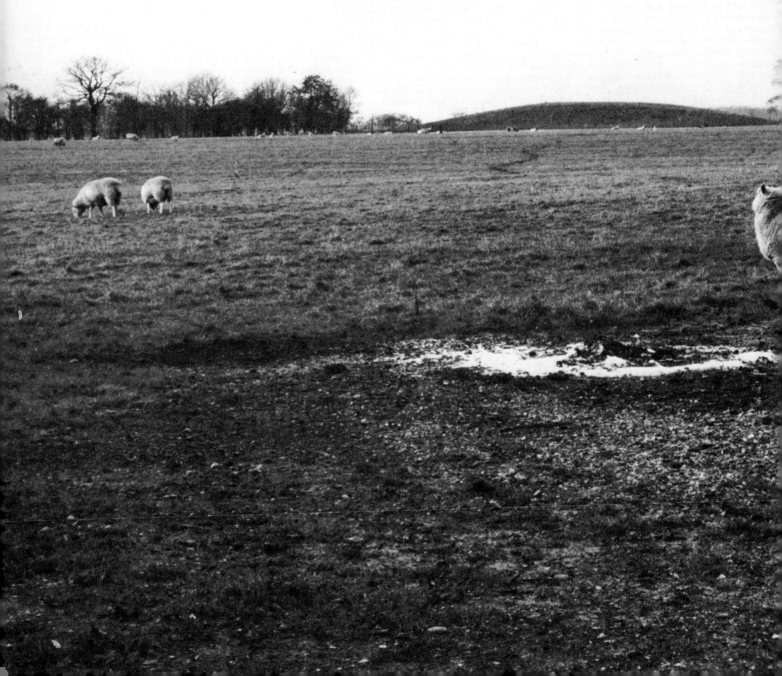

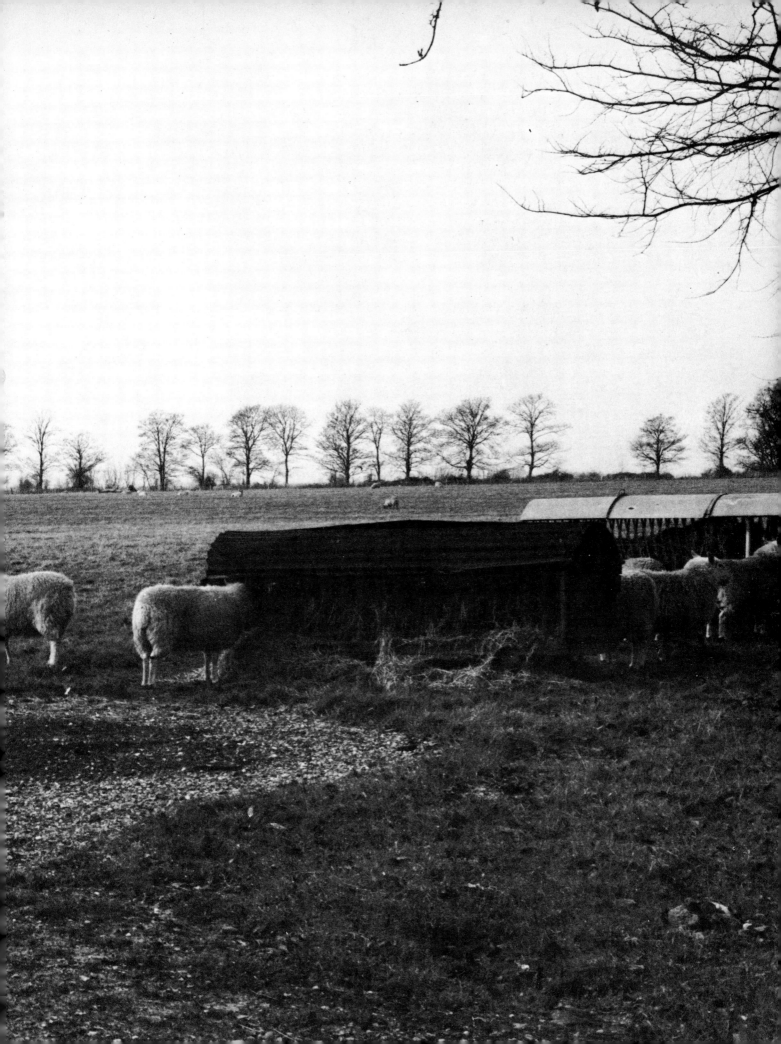

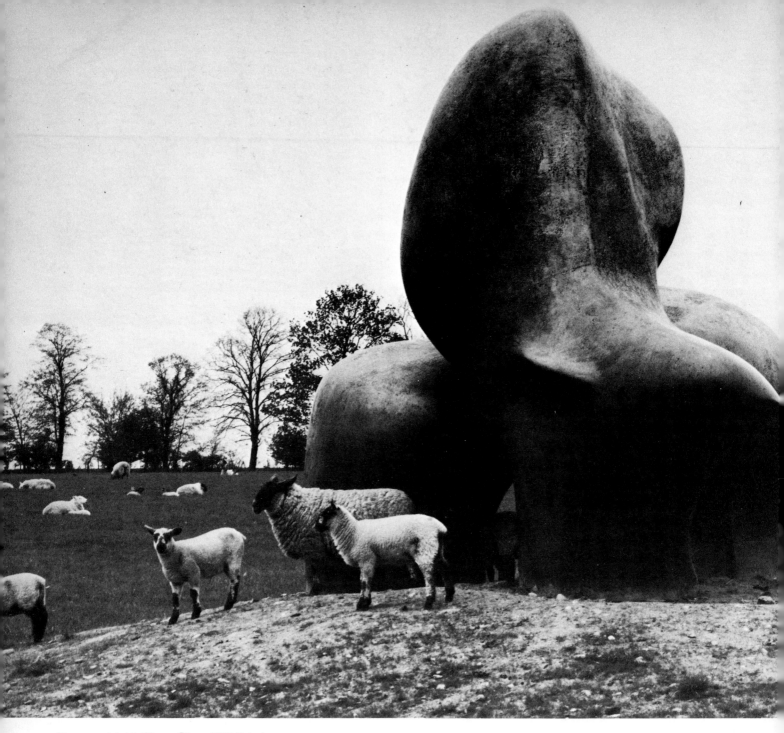

Above and right: *Sheep Piece* 1971/2, in bronze

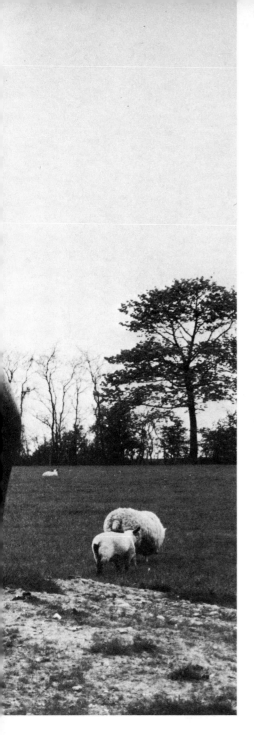

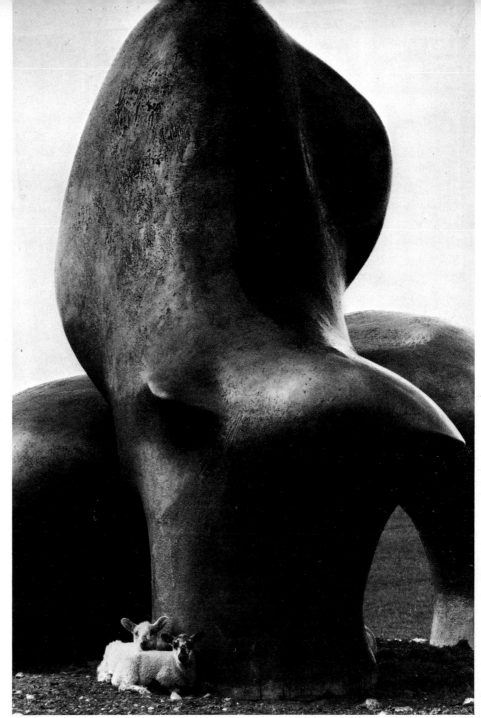

I think the fact that we have lived here since 1941 was very fortunate for me and for the development of my work. Gradually we were able to acquire further areas where I can place and relate my sculptures to the landscape. A local farmer friend grazes his sheep in these fields, which I like very much, because sheep are just the right scale to contrast with my sculptures – horses or cows are too big in scale. So, working on pieces like the *Sheep Piece,* and planning a sculpture for the small hill on the horizon, have been a great help in making sculptures to be seen in the open air.

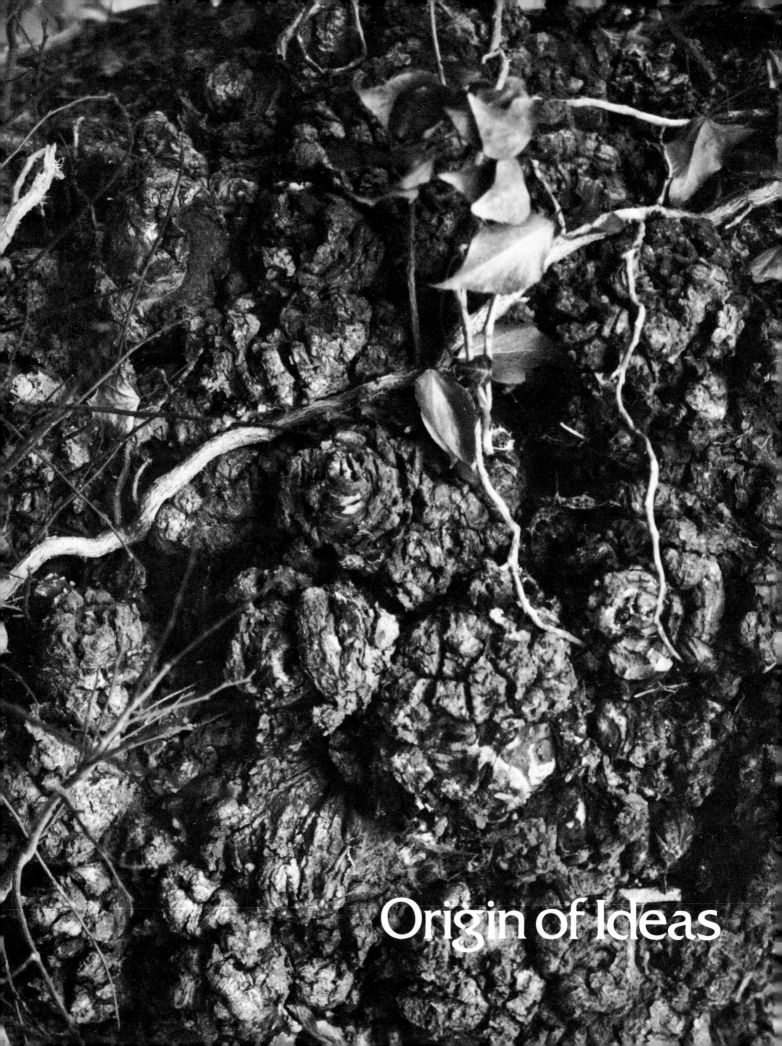

Origin of Ideas

I am a sculptor because the shape of things matters even more to me than the colour of them. It may be that a painter is excited as much by colour as by form. Some painters have been like this, though others have been as interested by form as sculptors are. For me, it is the three-dimensional reality and shape which one wants to understand, to grasp and to experience. This is, I think, what makes me a sculptor – I need these three dimensions, as a musician needs sound and notes of music, and a writer must be interested in words. The different arts call for a different sense – sight, touch, hearing, taste. The actual three dimensions of a form are what I like and need. I want to produce the complete thing, rather than a sketch or an illusion of it.

To understand real three dimensions is to train your mind to know when you see one view what it is like on the other side, to envelop it inside your head, as it were. This is not something that you are born with – a child has to learn how far away a toy is, hung up in its pram, by touching and feeling. We learn distances originally by walking them. We understand space through understanding form.

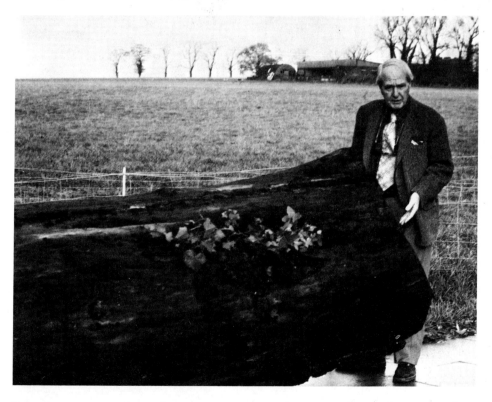

My large wood sculptures are mostly carved in elm wood because, in England, elm trees are the easiest to obtain in large, sound logs.

I intend one day to make a sculpture specially for this pool. I've made other sculptures which are placed in water, but they have architecture in the background. The sculpture here will be different.

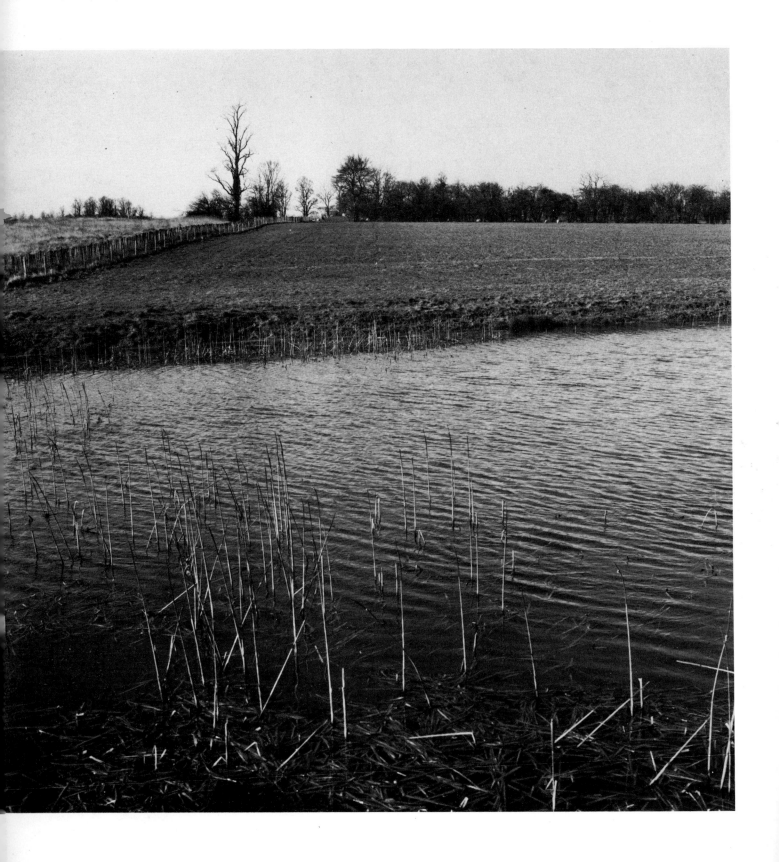

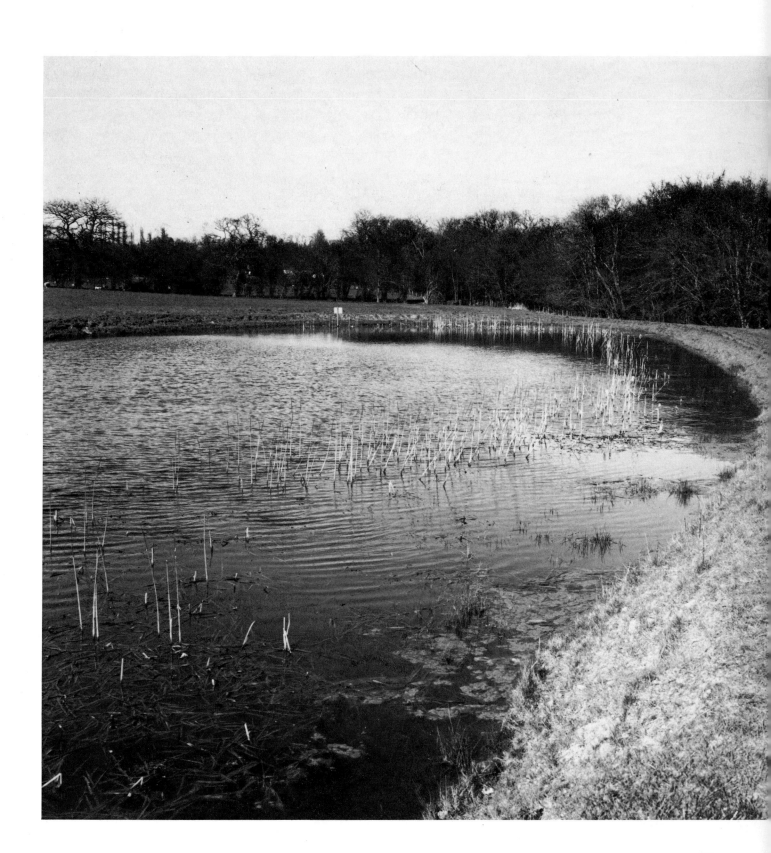

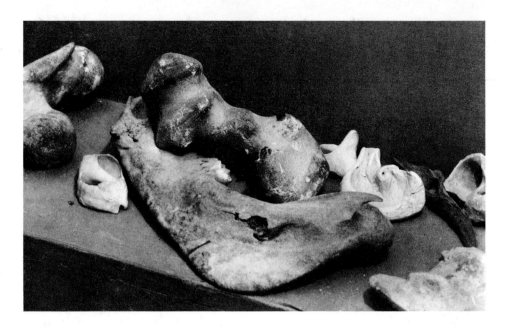

There is an infinite amount to be seen and enjoyed in the world – the texture of bark on trees, the shape of a shell, a nut, a plum, a pear, a tadpole, a mushroom, a mountain peak, a cloud, a kidney, a carrot, a tree trunk, a bird, a bull, a lark, a ladybird, a bulrush, a bone. Everything you think of has its own individual, unified idea of form.

For me, everything in the world of form is understood through our own bodies. From our mother's breast, from our bones, from bumping into things, we learn what is rough and what is smooth. To observe, to understand, to experience the vast variety of space, shape and form in the world, twenty lifetimes would not be enough. There is no end to it.

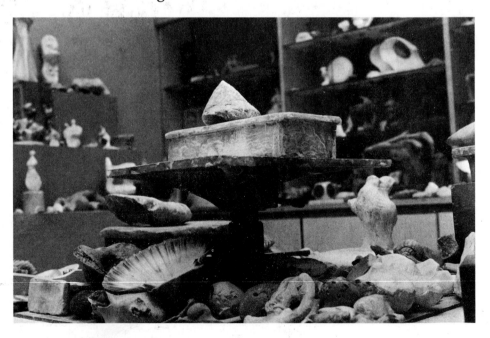

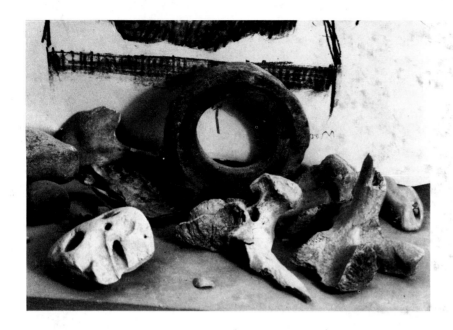

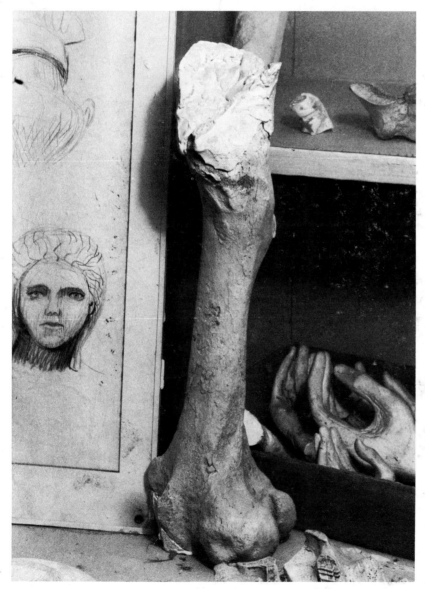

Left and opposite:
Bones, shells and other found-objects in one
of Henry Moore's maquette studios

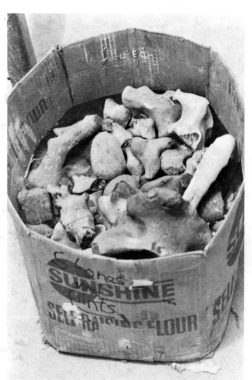

A box of flints and pebbles

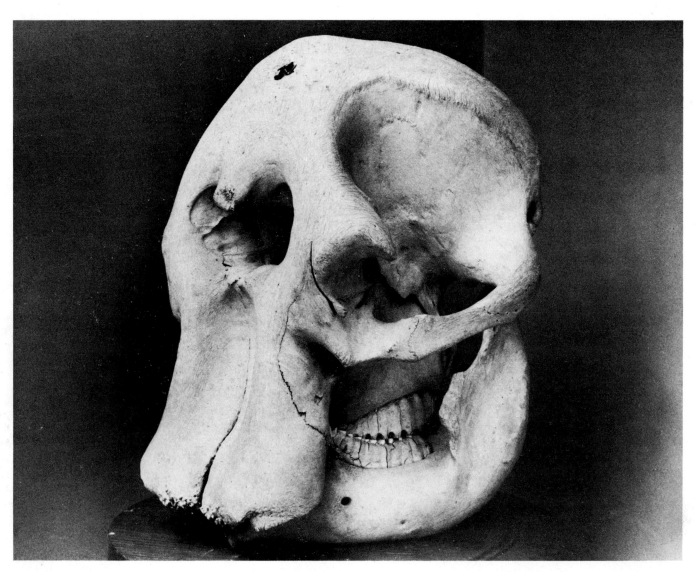

Elephant skull

The elephant skull was given to my old friend, the late Sir Julian Huxley, on one of his visits to Africa. He kept it in his garden in Hampstead, where it was deteriorating in the weather. He knew that I was interested in the shape of bones, so he made a gift of it to me. I gladly accepted it, for I don't know of another single bone unit with such a variety of forms within it – it is, for instance, much more complex than a human skull. I have made many drawings of the skull, and an album of more than thirty etchings showing different views and sections of it. It would be easy to find as many other views to draw.

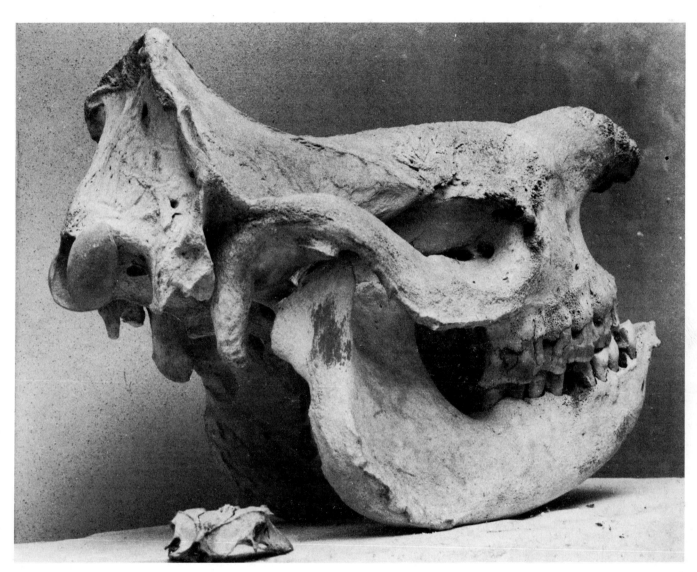

Sir Julian gave me the rhinoceros skull at the same time as the
elephant skull. Its form has great interest, but it does not appeal
to me as much as the elephant skull. It has a ferocious,
aggressive character, whereas the elephant skull, although
powerful, gives an impression of gentleness and serenity.

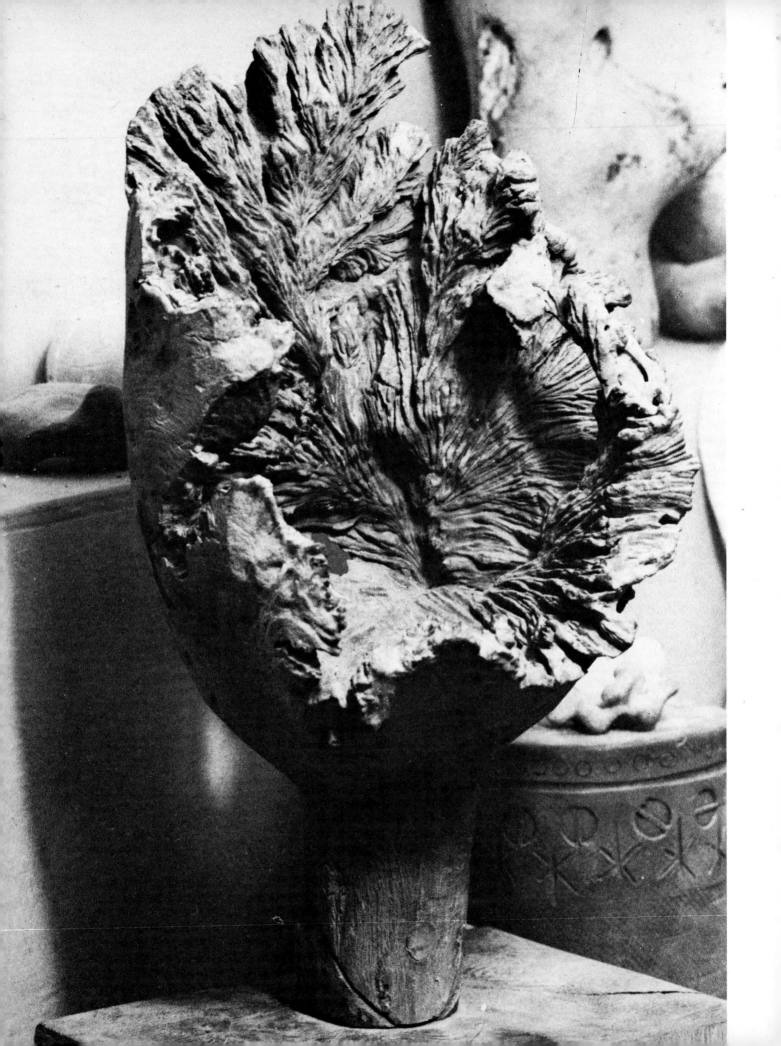

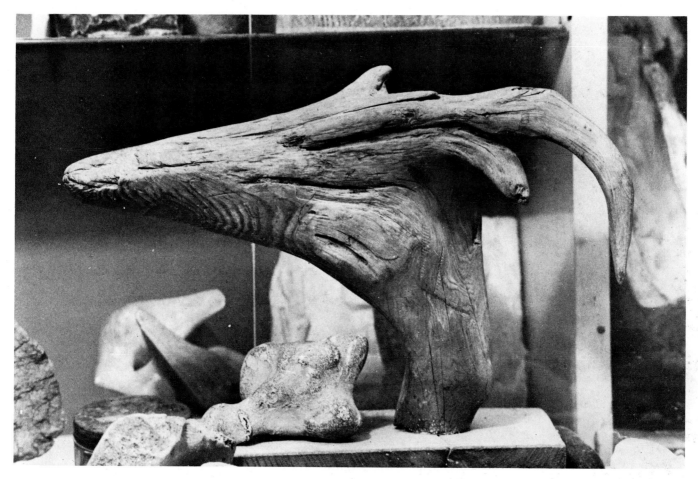

Anything and everything in the world – pebbles, bones, shells – all can give principles about form. A shell is a hard form that nature makes to protect something soft and vulnerable inside it. Bones are the hard, inner structure supporting a soft, outer form. As a boy I looked at, played with and collected wood, sticks and bones, and my studio is now full of examples. This finding of nature has grown in the last forty or fifty years and many people now probably look at things in which they would never have had the faintest interest before, and this all makes the world a more interesting place.

Below: Maquette studio and (opposite) shelves of plaster maquettes and found-objects

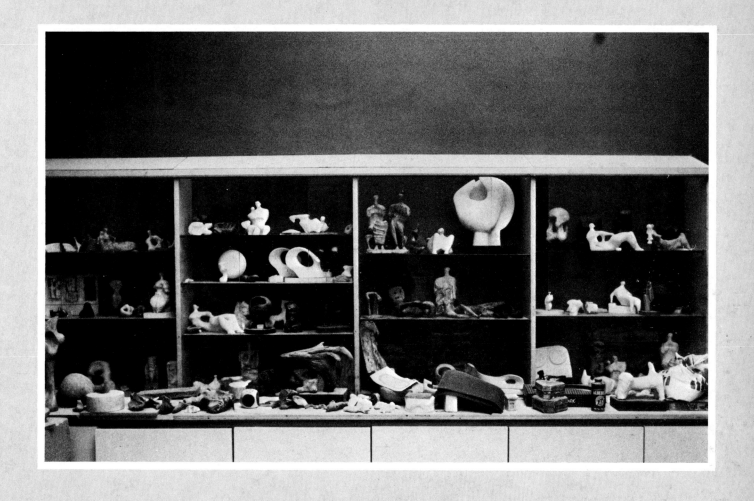

Inside the Studio

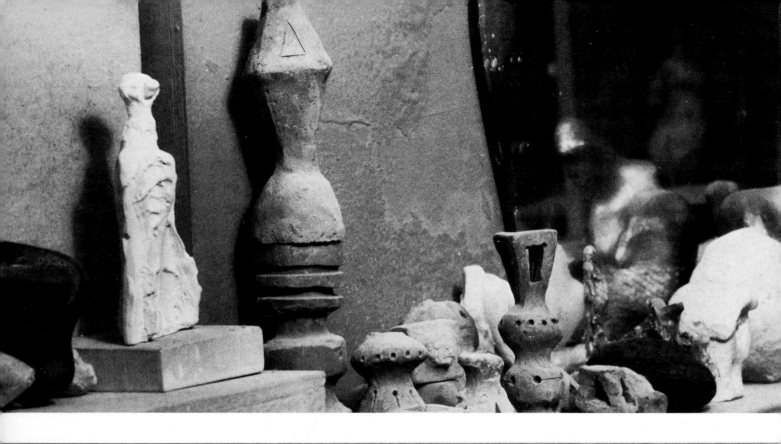
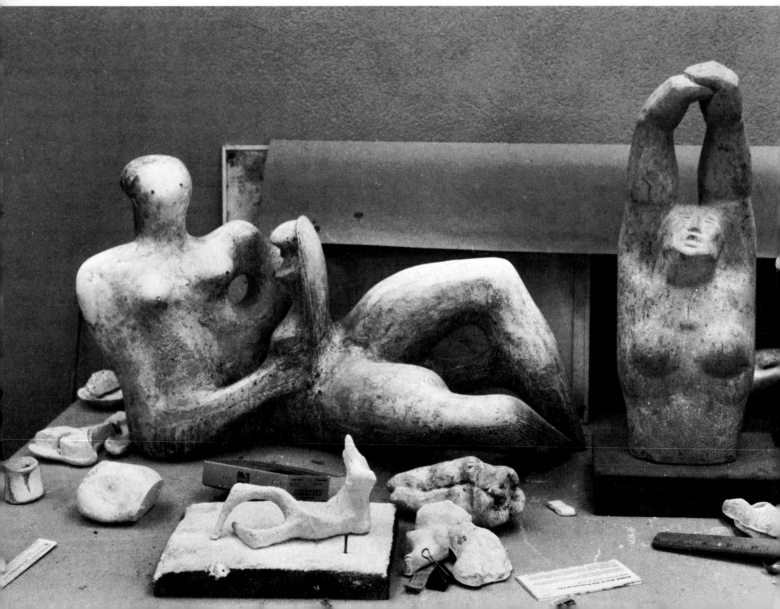

Left above: Preliminary clay maquettes for *Bird Table* 1954, in terracotta

Left below: Table in the corner of the Gildmore maquette studio with *Working Model for Reclining Mother and Child* 1974/5, in plaster. In the foreground, the plaster model of *Reclining Figure: Crossed Legs* and, to the right, an early carving, *Woman with Upraised Arms* 1924/5, in Hopton-wood stone

Below: Maquettes, and marble *Head* still in unfinished state

Sometimes I make ten or twenty maquettes for every one that I use in a large scale – the others may get rejected. If a maquette keeps its interest enough for me to want to realise it as a full-size final work, then I might make a working model in an intermediate size, in which changes will be made before going to the real, full-sized sculpture. Changes get made at all these stages.

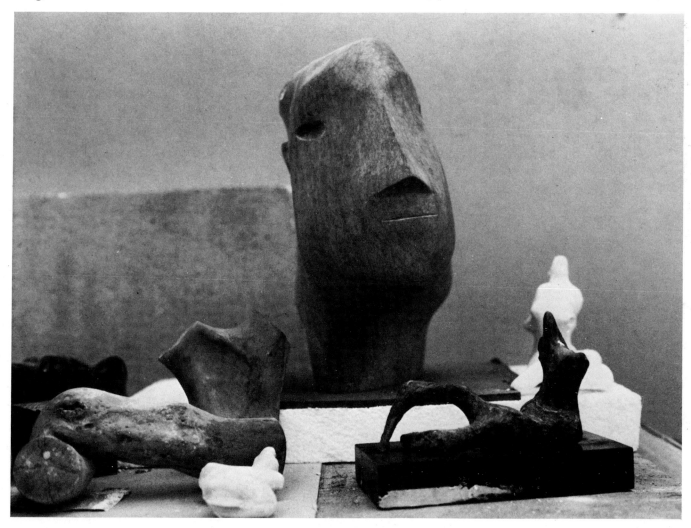

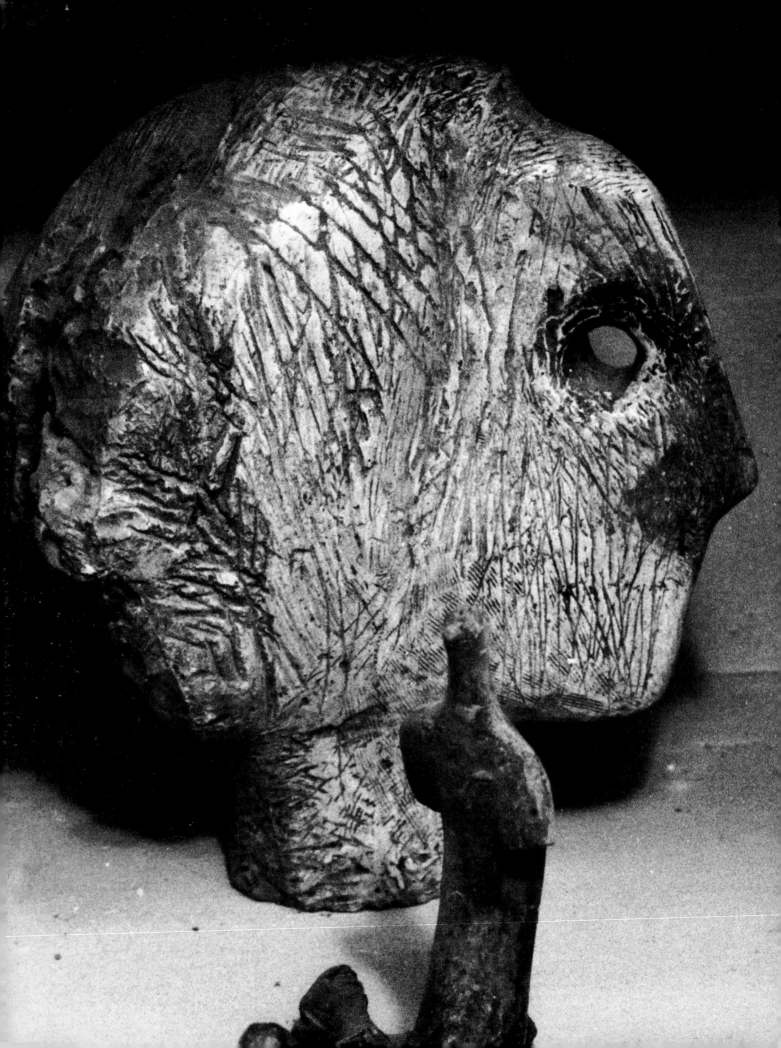

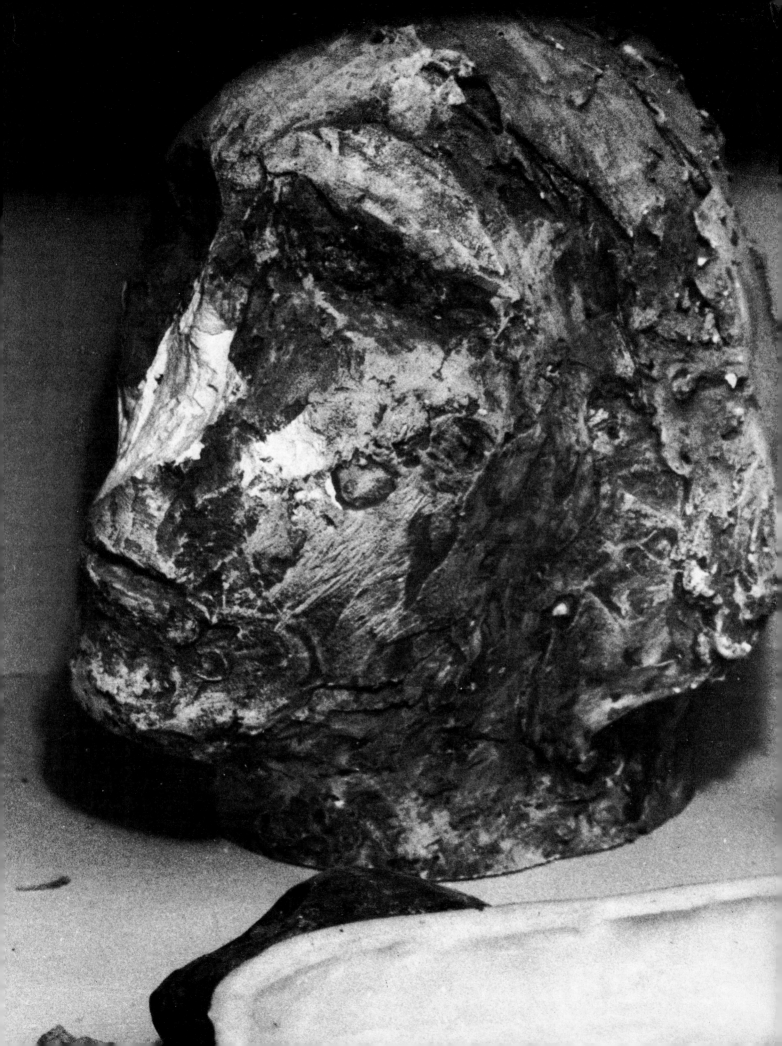

Previous pages: Two plaster heads: on the left, one of the trials for the head of the Queen in *King and Queen* 1952; on the right, a trial for one of the heads carved for the porch of the parish church of Much Hadham

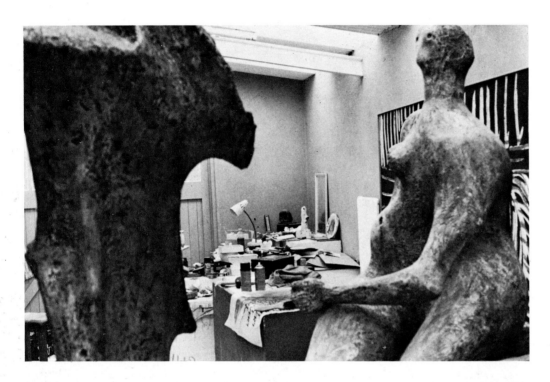

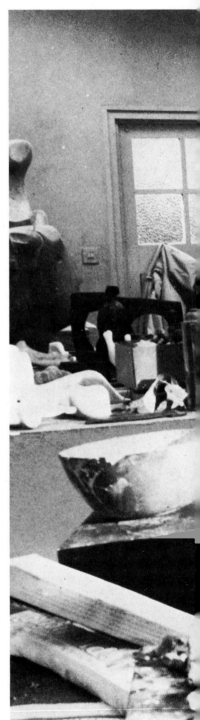

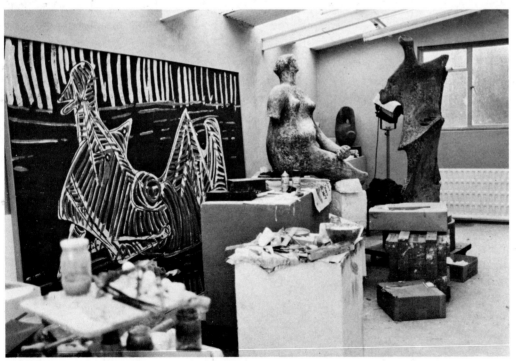

Left above: A corner of the Gildmore maquette studio with, in the foreground, details of the original plasters for *Working Model for Standing Figure: Knife Edge* 1961, and *Seated Woman* 1957

Left below: Another view of the same studio and plasters, also showing the silk-screen panel, *Reclining Figure,* printed on linen in 1947

Below: Henry Moore at work in the Gildmore maquette studio

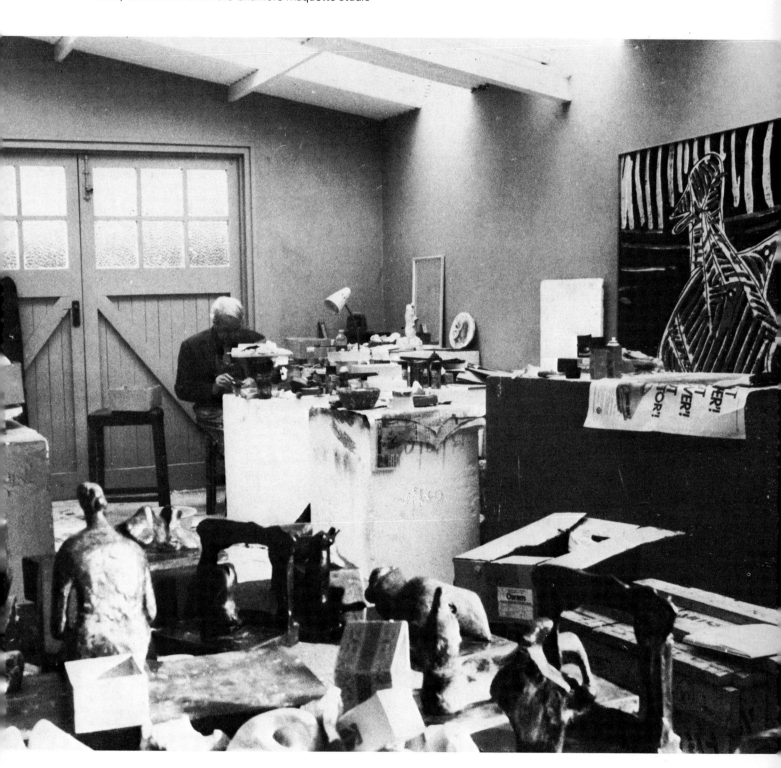

As a young sculptor, I just had one studio. I had no studio in my
student days, and used to carve in my parents' garden in the
holidays. That might have led to my liking working
out-of-doors, and seeing sculpture out-of-doors too. Until I
could afford to have two studios, if I wanted to draw, I would
work in the same studio as I did my sculpture. Doing a drawing
of any size, I would have to clear a space in my studio. When I
went back to the sculpture, there would be another
interruption.

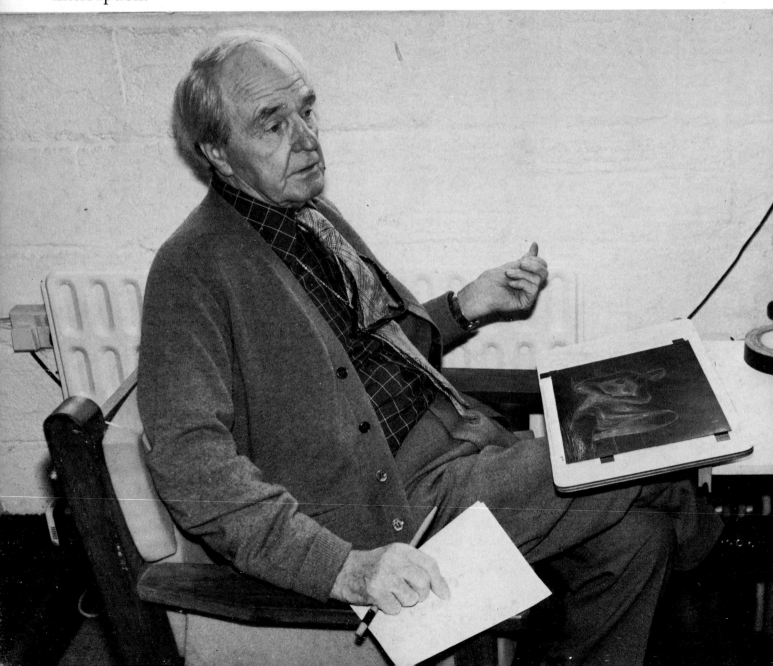

Following pages: Henry Moore in the Gildmore graphic studio during the making of a film on his drawings by John Read for BBC TV

When our housekeeper moved into Gildmore, the house next door, I used its studio for my drawing and lithography. I painted the walls white and put a carpet on the floor, which has made it a pleasant place to work in. By putting screens in, I can hang my lithographs, to see if I need to do any further work on them. I couldn't have done this in the old days, when I had to clear a space in my sculpture studio.

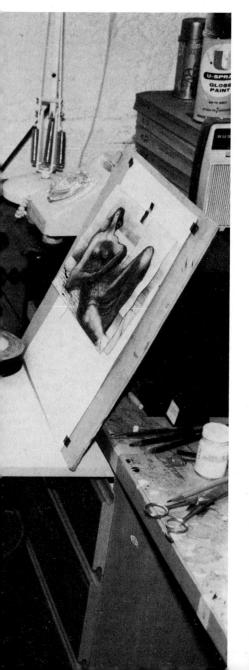

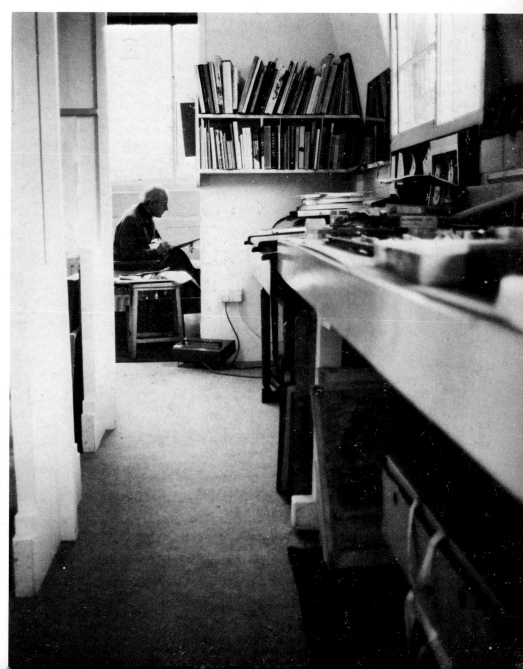

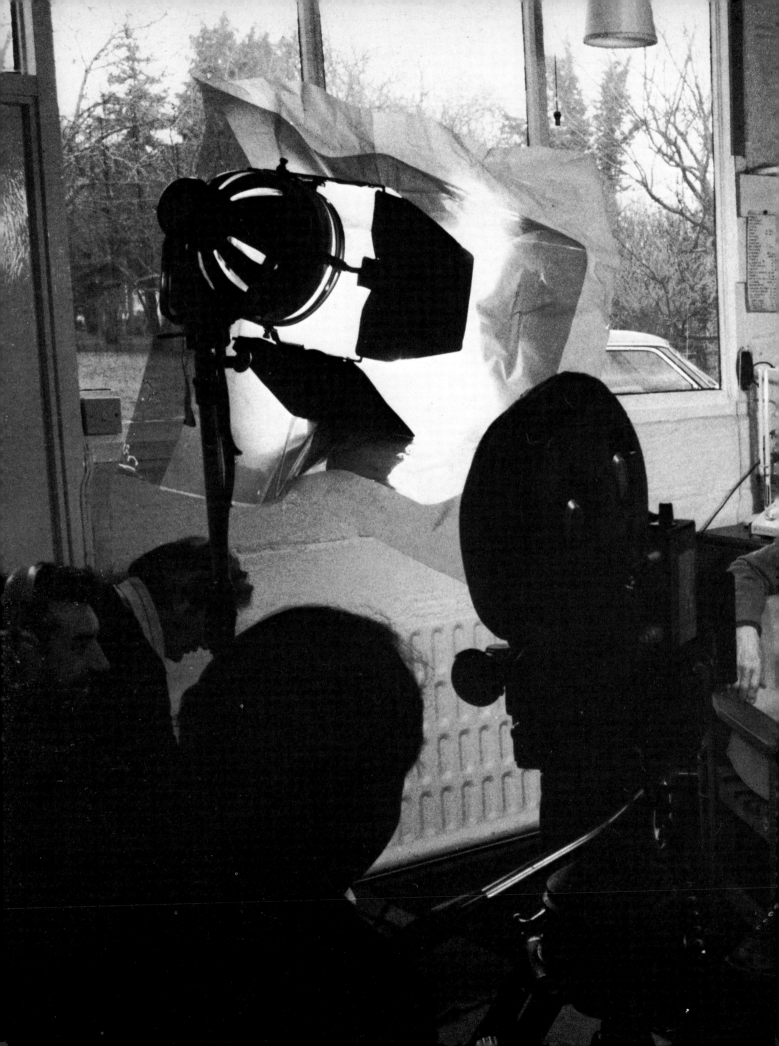

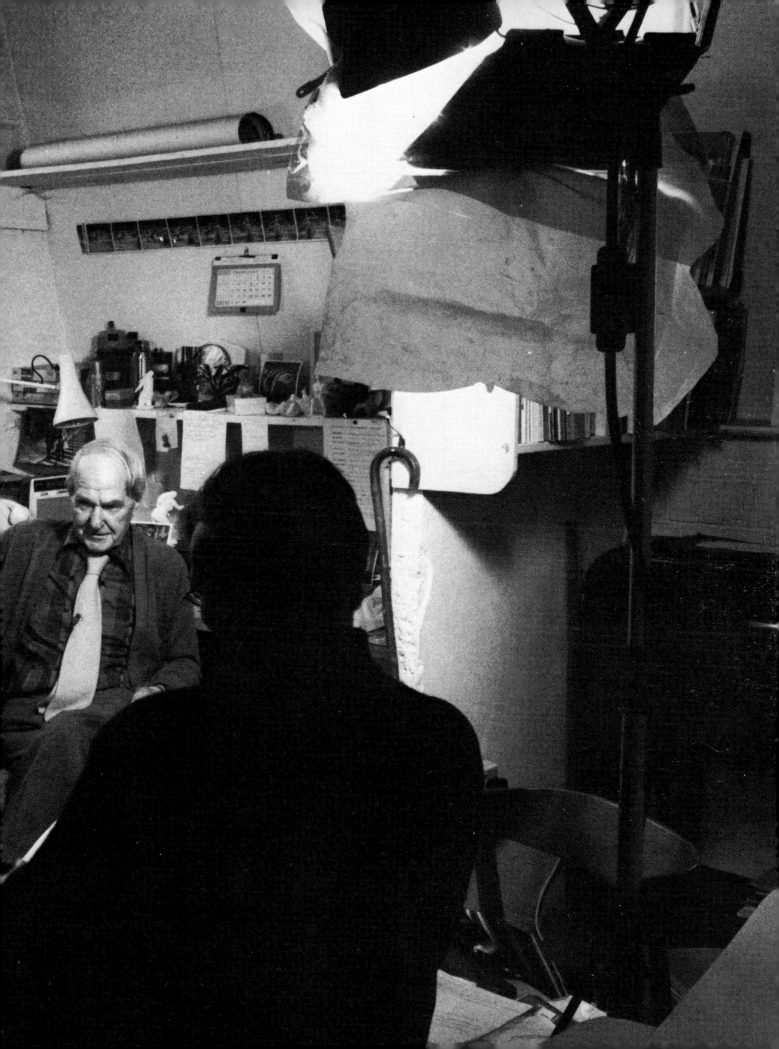

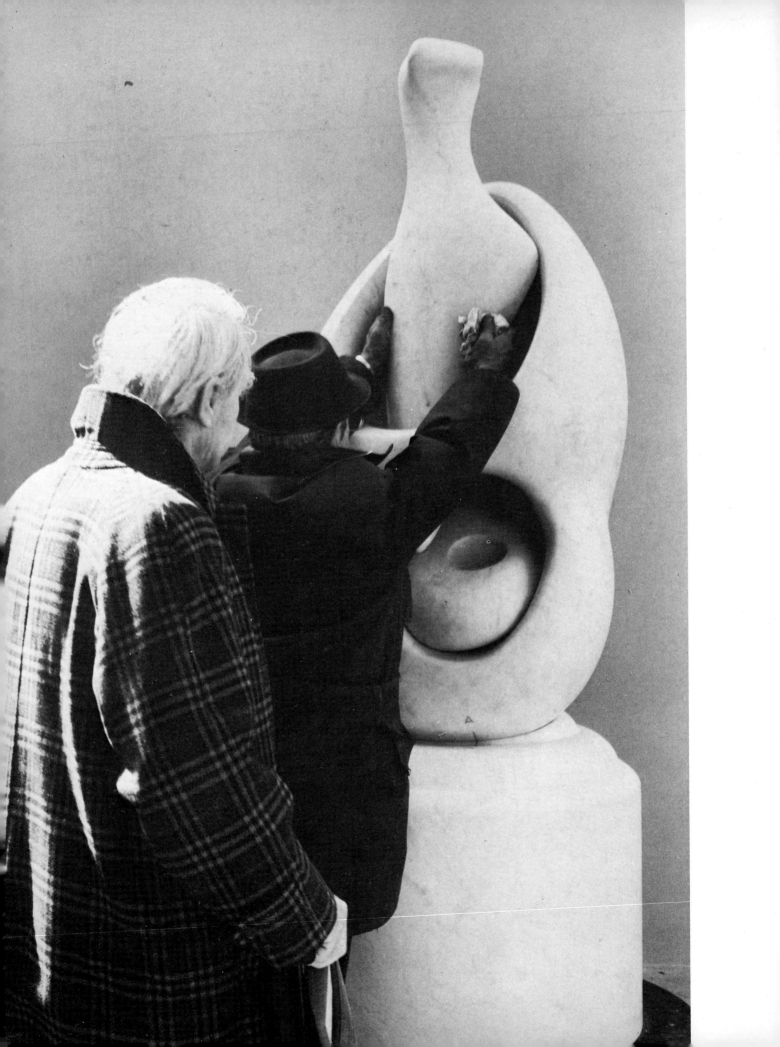

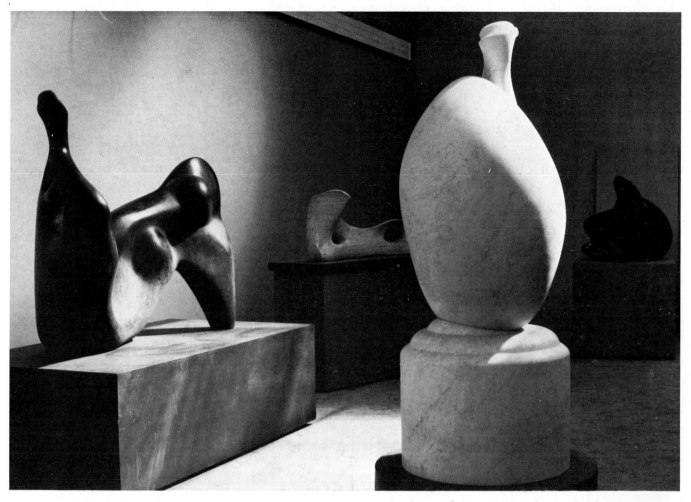

I am now making a studio which I consider suitable for showing my carvings, mainly those from the last ten or twelve years. In this studio, I have tried to have a general light which is equally good in all areas. For sculpture one needs a 'plastic' lighting – that is, lighting that shows the shape that is the modelling of the form. In principle, the maximum plasticity is shown when the direction of the light is at right angles to the line of vision. Take, for example, a back light: a sculpture directly in front of a window comes out as a silhouette, you see only an outline of a mass. A dead front light is equally unsatisfactory because it flattens the form. Flashlight photographs show what I mean, the object looking as though it has been whitewashed.

A top light – a light coming from above, the sky or a sky light – is at right angles to one's horizontal vision, and so the light coming from it strikes the object at right angles to the viewer's horizontal vision, and therefore gives the maximum modelling to the form. A studio with a top light throughout can have many more works getting equally good 'plastic' lighting.

Opposite: Henry Moore and Frank Farnham fixing the interior units of *Mother and Child: Egg Form* 1977 in white marble

Above: Dane Tree House Gallery with, on the left, *Reclining Figure: Single Leg* 1976, in black marble, behind *Reclining Figure: Bone* 1975, in Roman travertine, *Reclining Figure: Curved* 1977 in black marble, and back view of *Mother and Child: Egg Form* 1977 in white marlbe

Following pages: Henry Moore with Don Schooling and Frank Farnham, looking at the first carvings to be moved into the new gallery attached to Dane Tree House. On the left, *Mother and Child: Egg Form,* and on the right, *Reclining Figure: Single Leg* 1976, in black marble

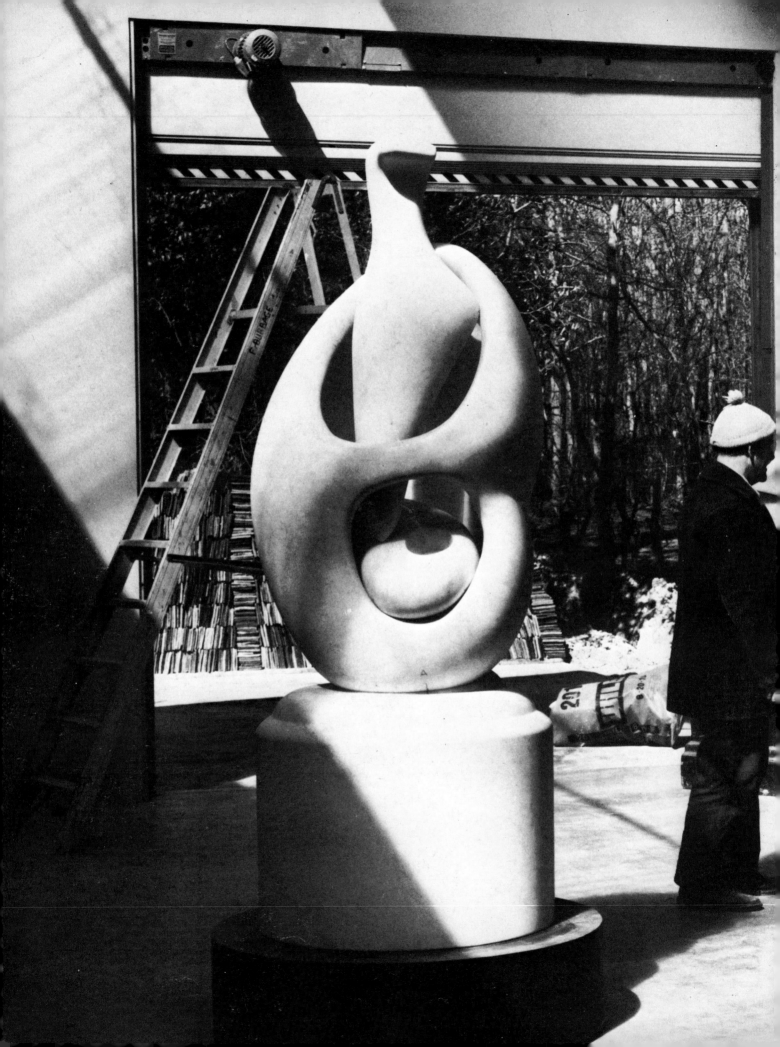

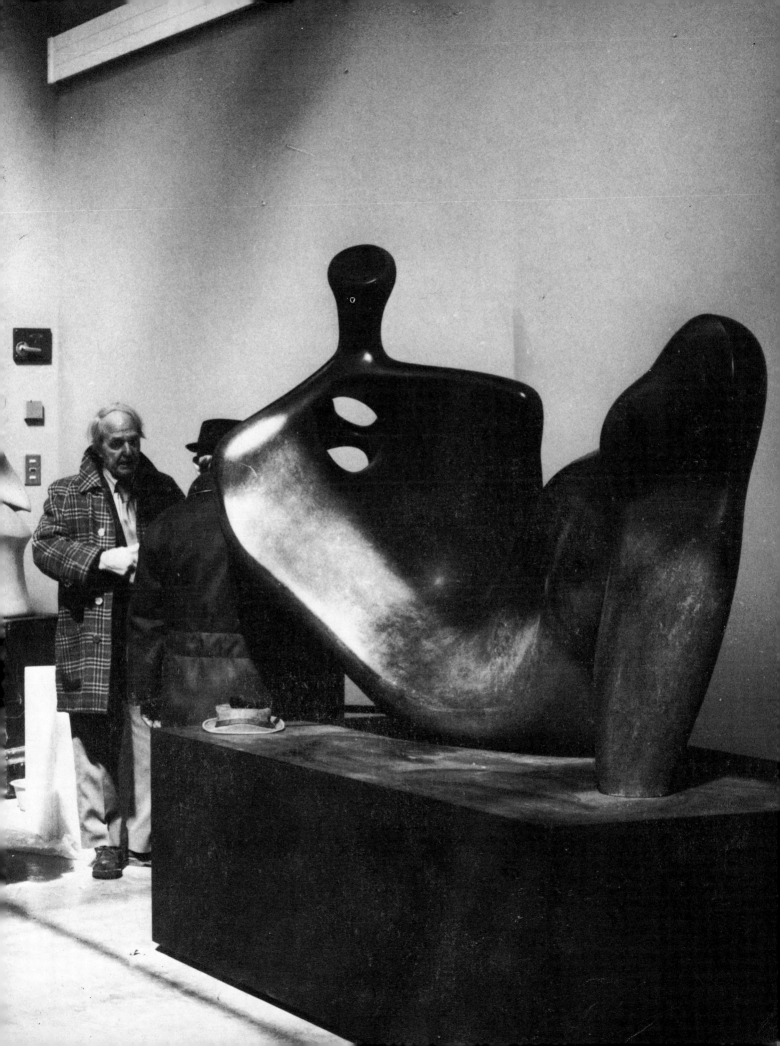

The original studio nearest the house, now called the Top Studio.
In the foreground, *Draped Reclining Figure* 1976, in bronze

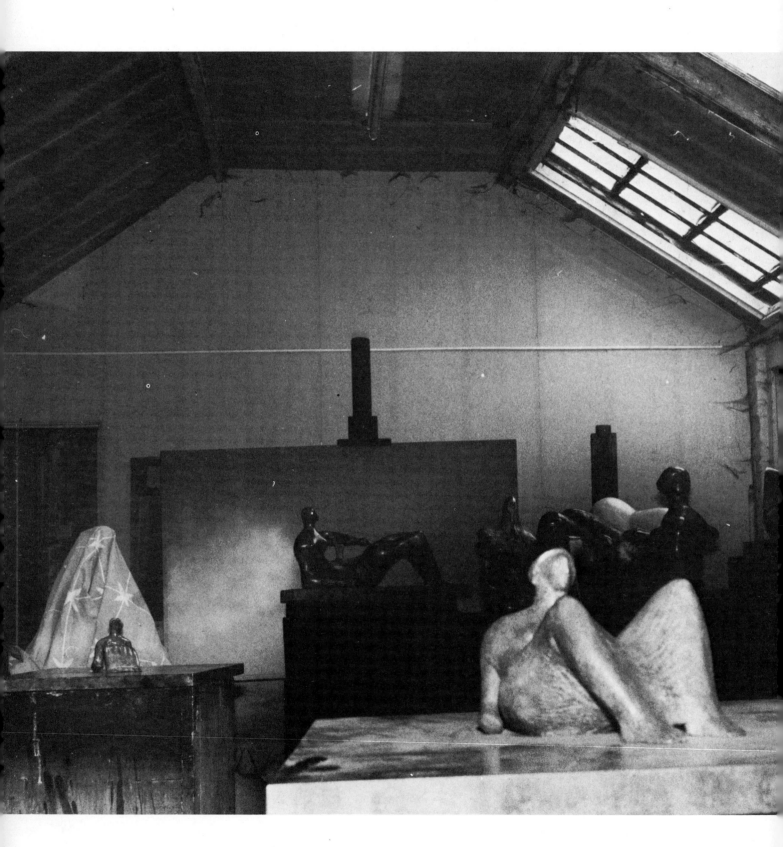

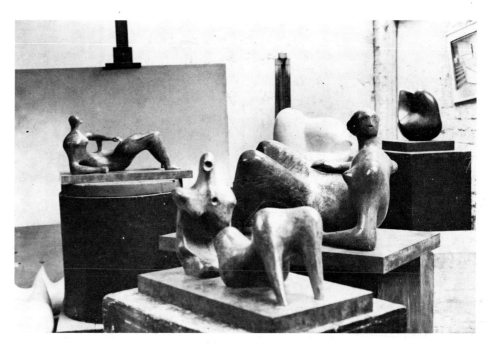

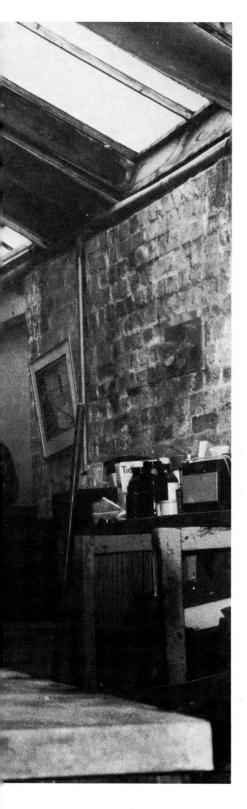

Up till now, my studios have been made mainly for working in. Providing there was part of the studio with good daylight to work by, the rest of the studio could be used for storage, and so on. The exception to this is the Plastic Studio which is specially used for large sculptures, intended to be seen out-of-doors.

Opposite; The artist with the fibre-glass cast of *the arch* 1963/69

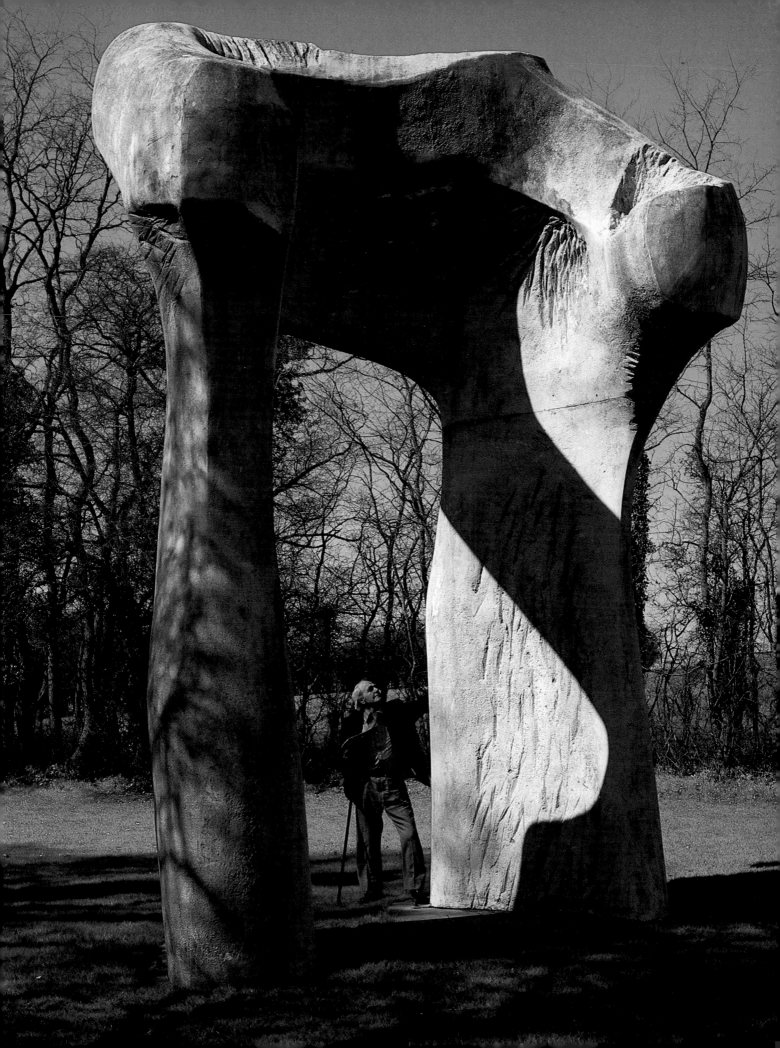

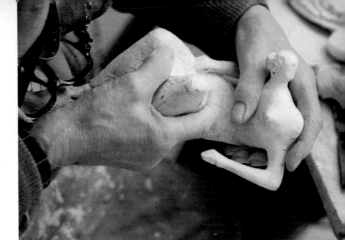

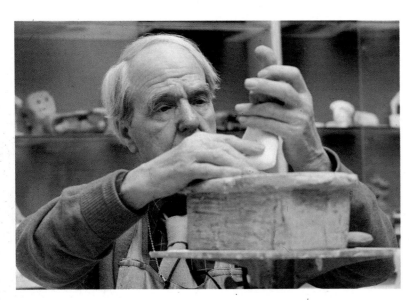

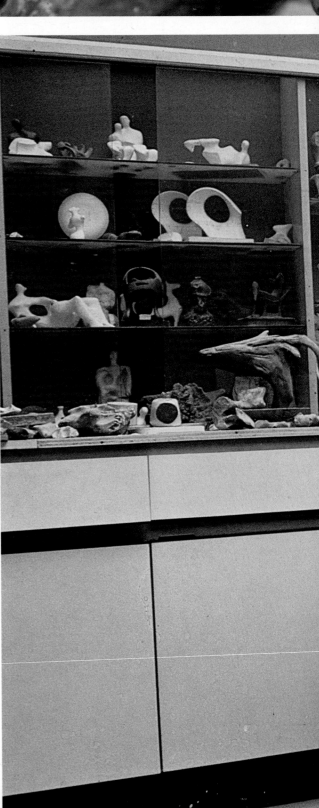

Moore working in his maquette studio

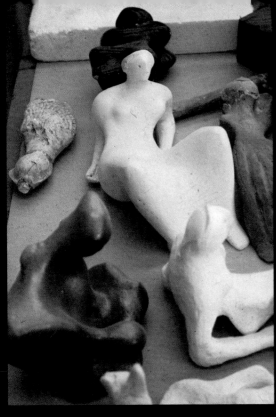

Left and below: Plaster maquettes of reclining figures and a
mother and child
Opposite above: Sculptor's tools on a polystyrene block
Opposite below: Top Studio with *Bird Form II* 1973, in black
marble, and *Seated Torso* 1954, in bronze

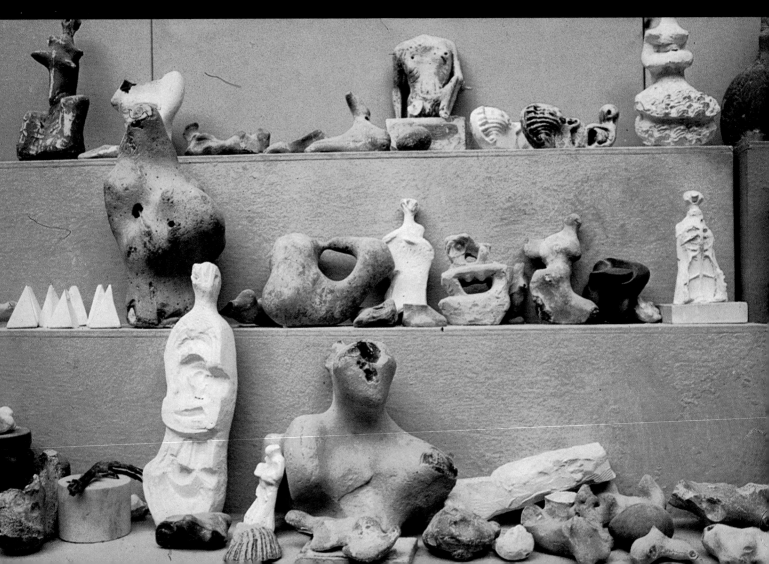

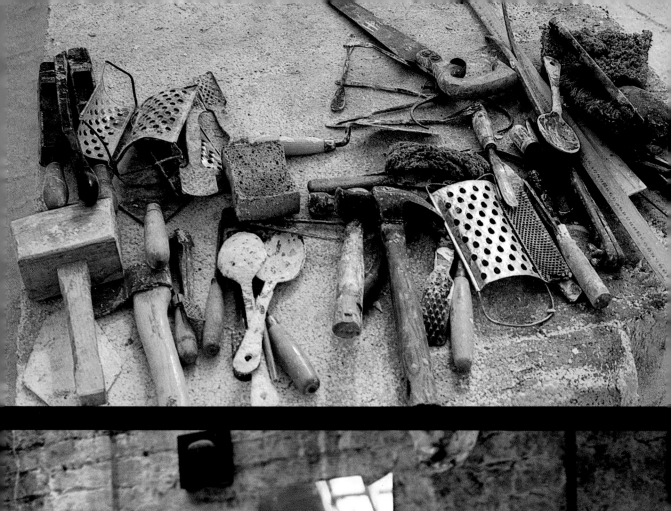

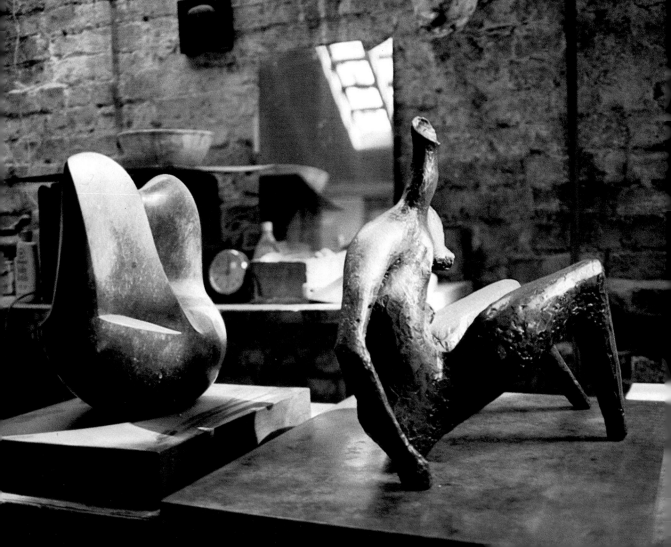

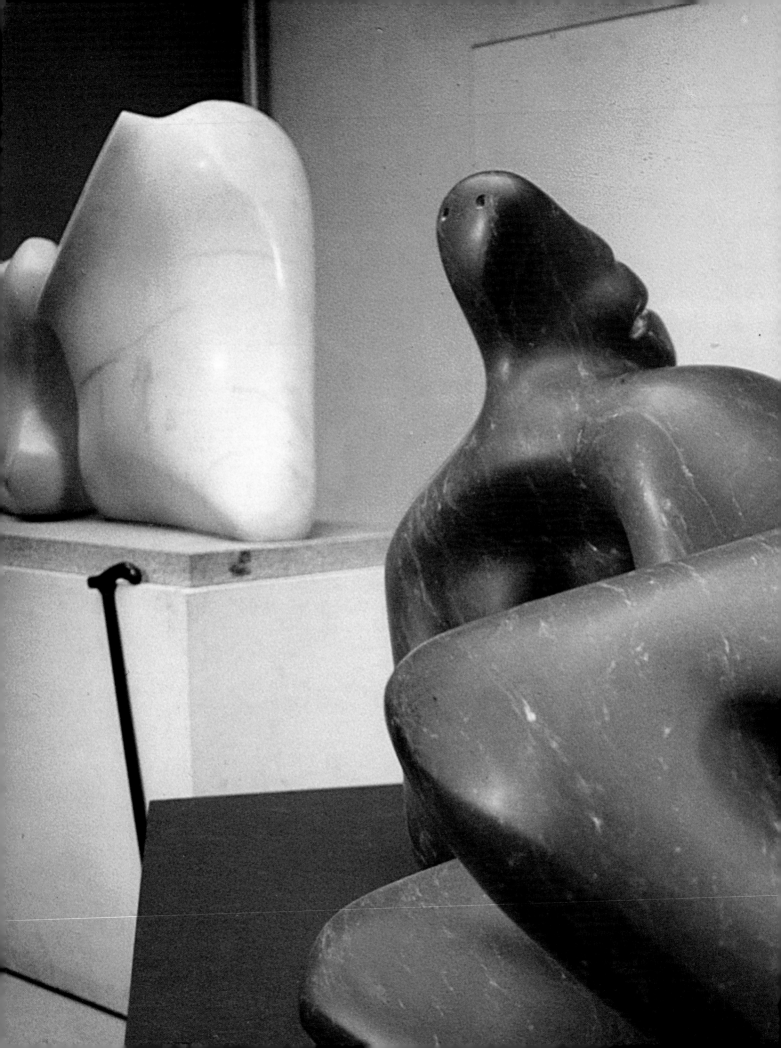

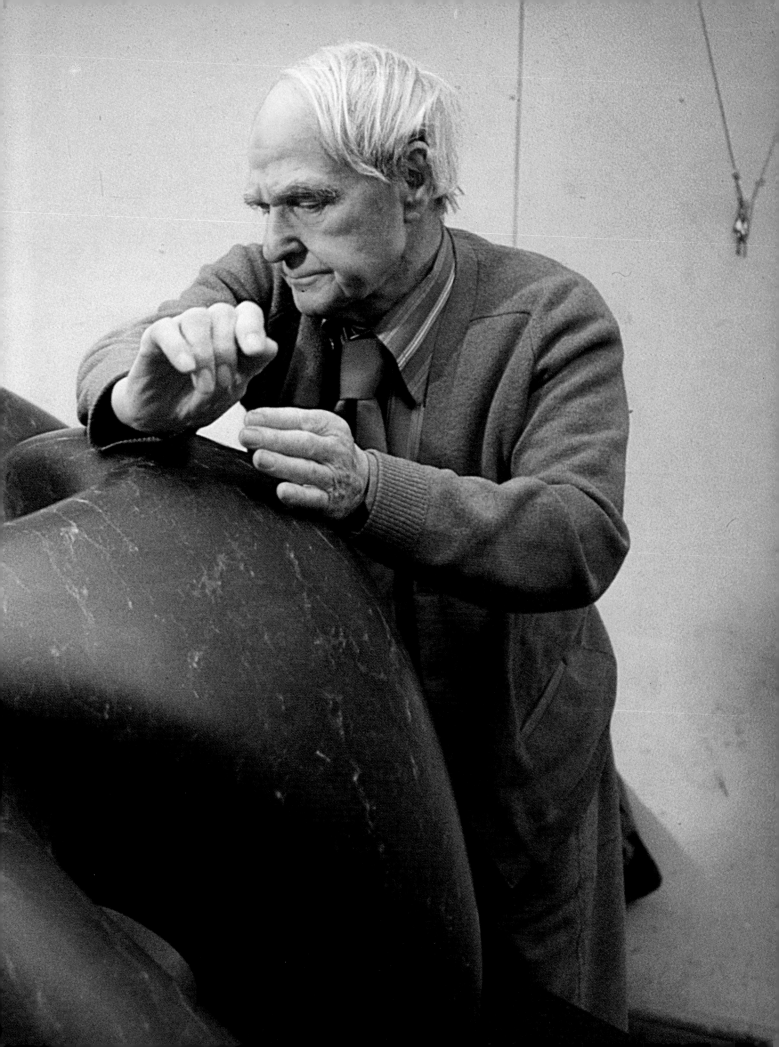

Previous pages: Henry Moore with *Reclining Figure: Curved* 1977, in
black marble, and, in the background, *Mother and Child* 1967, in rosa
aurora
Below: Henry Moore working with an etching needle on a prepared
copper plate
Bottom: The artist looking through a recent sketch book
Centre: In the Gildmore Studio, an early proof of the lithograph *Mother and
Child Ideas and Reclining Figure* 1977

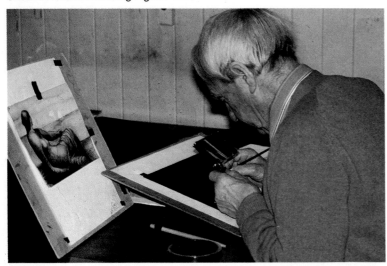

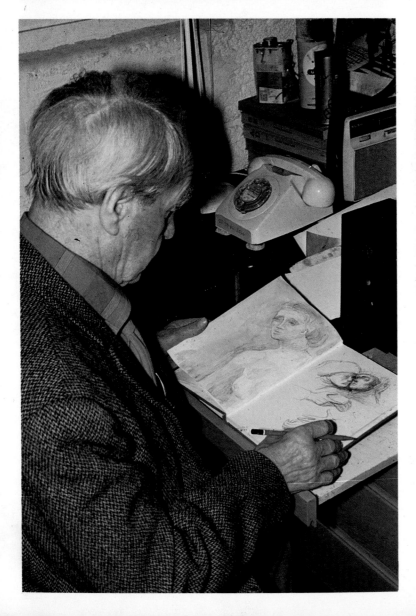

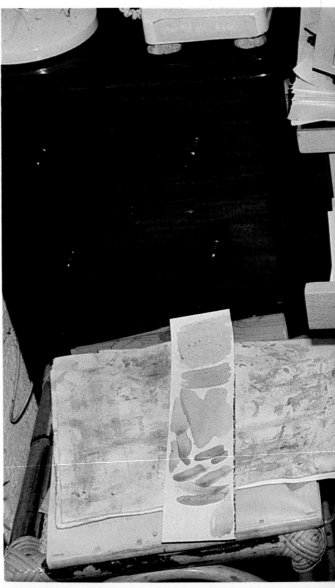

Below: A group of objects on the sitting room table
Bottom: Basket with gourds, a sea urchin and an ostrich egg

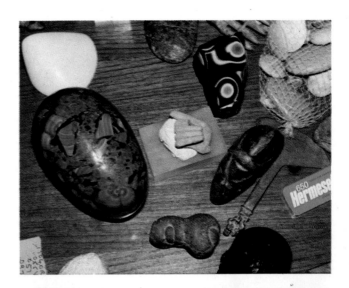

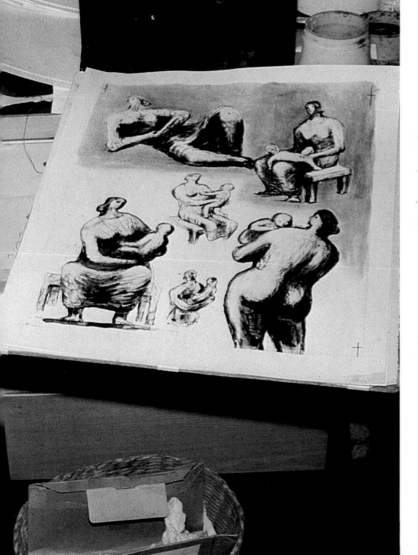

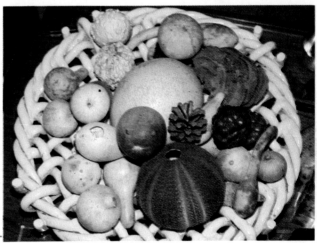

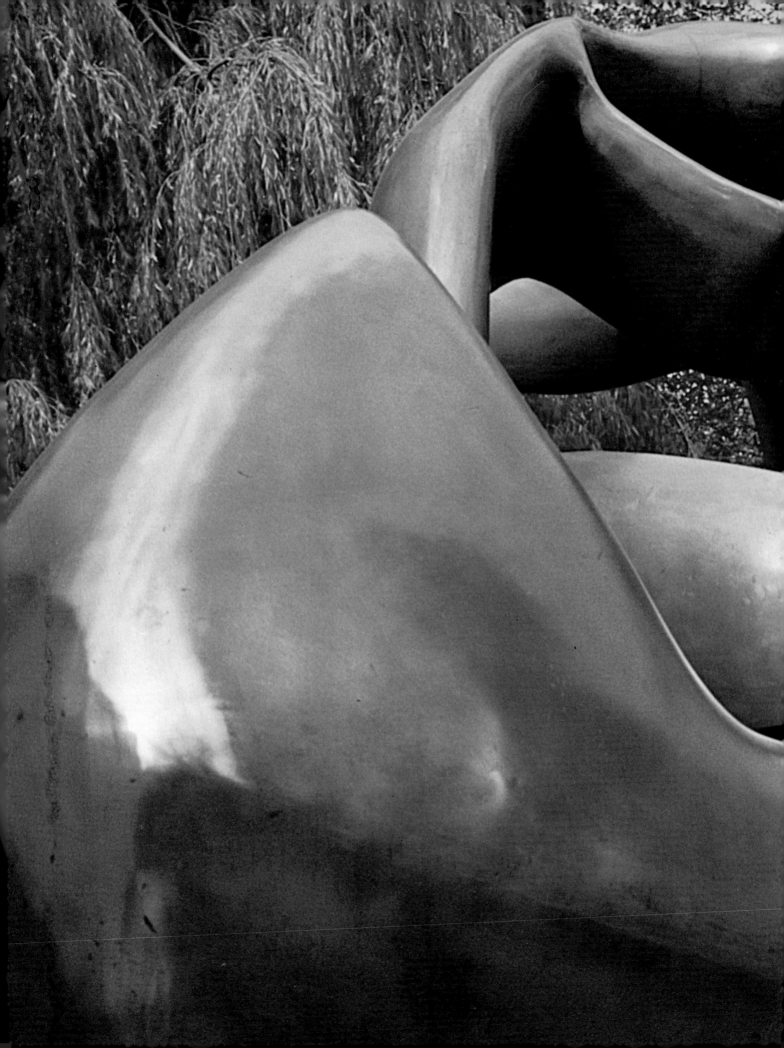

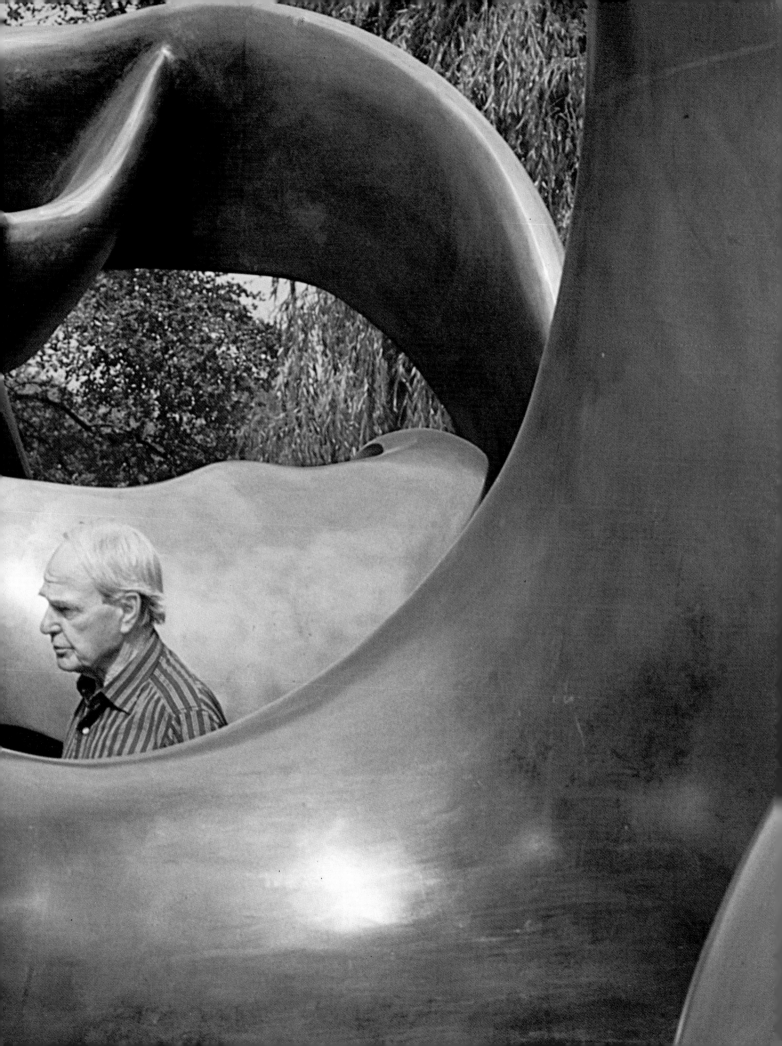

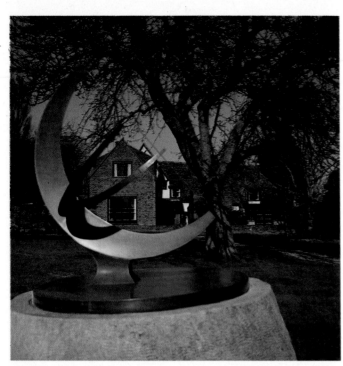

Previous pages: The sculptor seen through the *Hill Arches* 1973, in bronze
Left: *Working Model for Sundial* 1965, in bronze, with Hoglands in the background
Below: The garden at Hoglands

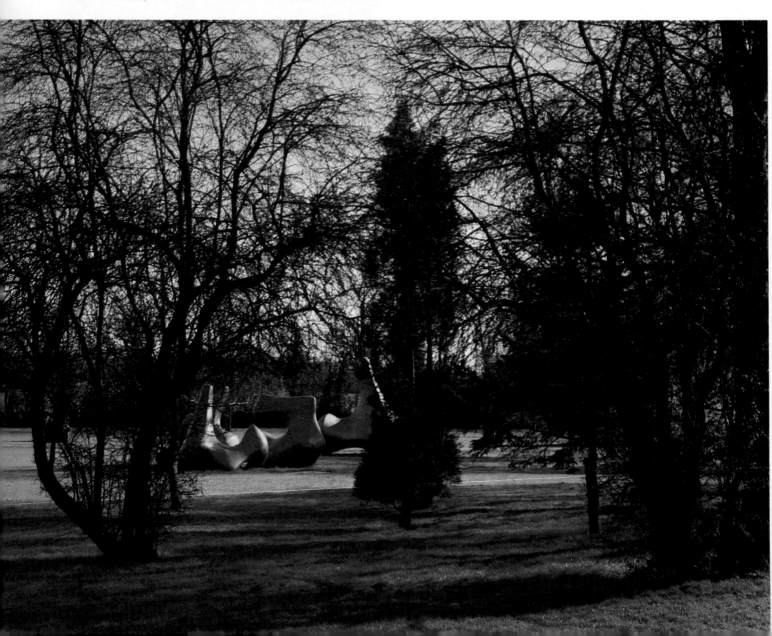

Right: Roofs of Hoglands
Below: View of the garden

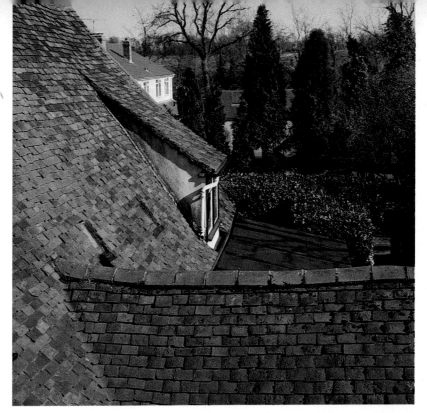

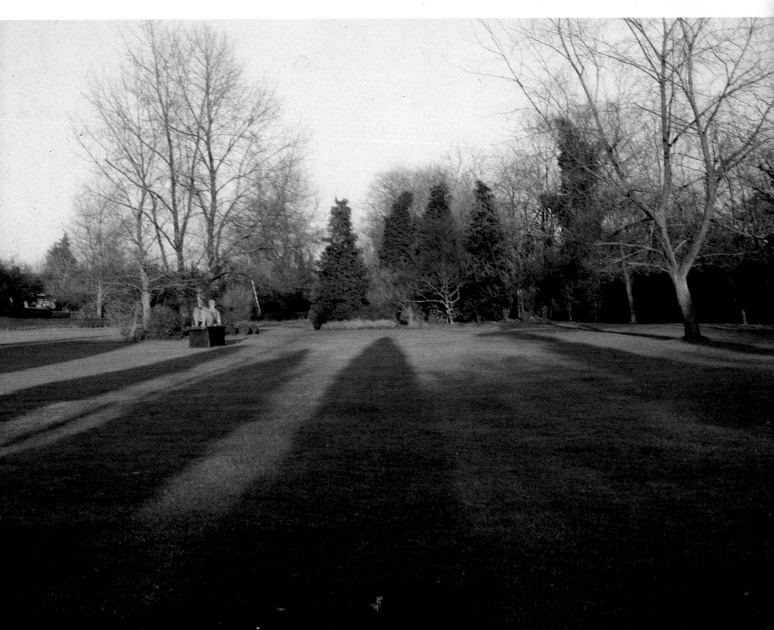

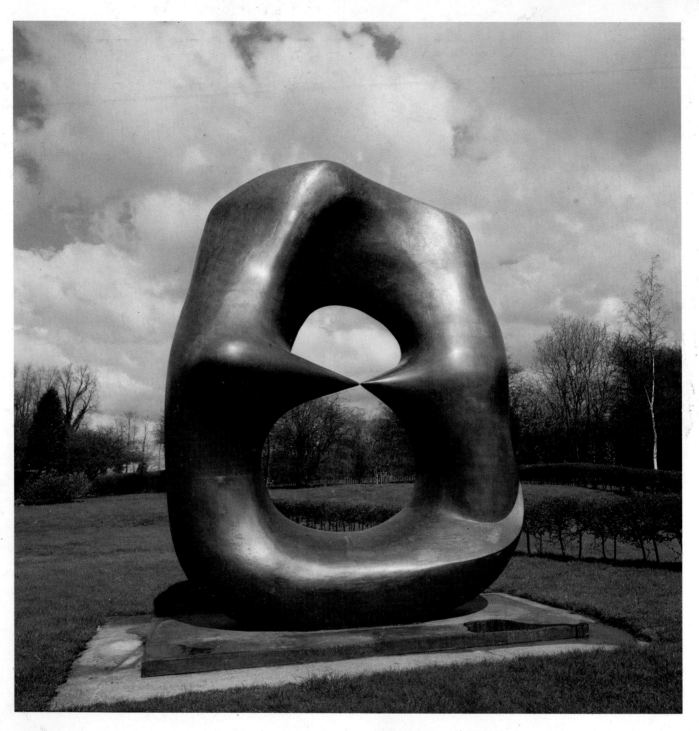

Oval with Points 1968/70, in bronze
Opposite: Henry Moore looking at head end of *Three Piece
Reclining Figure: Draped* 1975, in bronze

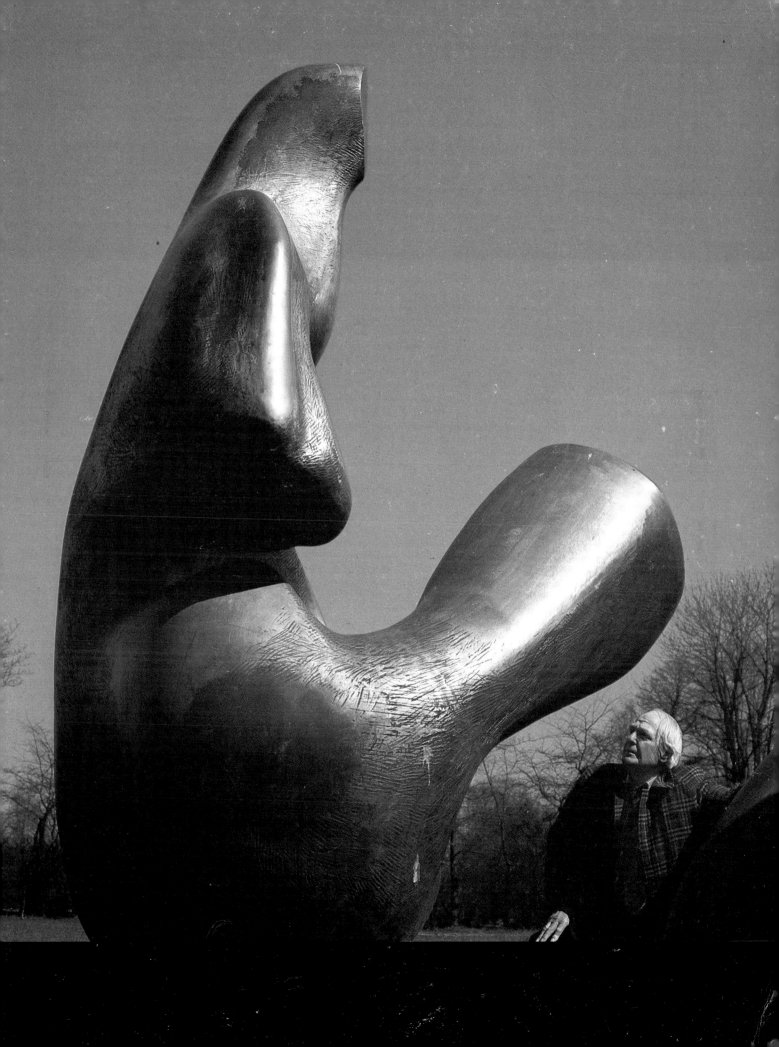

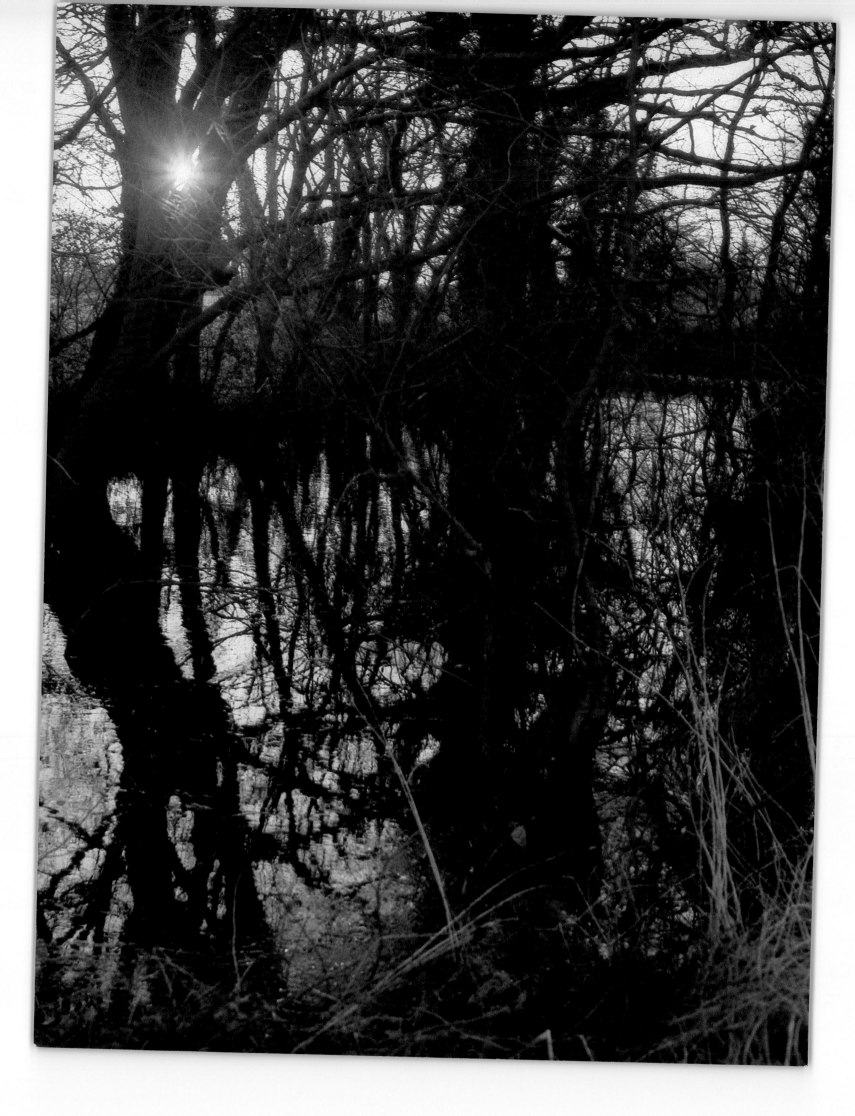

Opposite; The Hertfordshire countryside

Below: In the foreground, *Working Model for Mirror Knife Edge* 1976, in bronze
Bottom: Bronze cast of *Reclining Figure: Bone Skirt* 1977, ready to be sent to its new owner

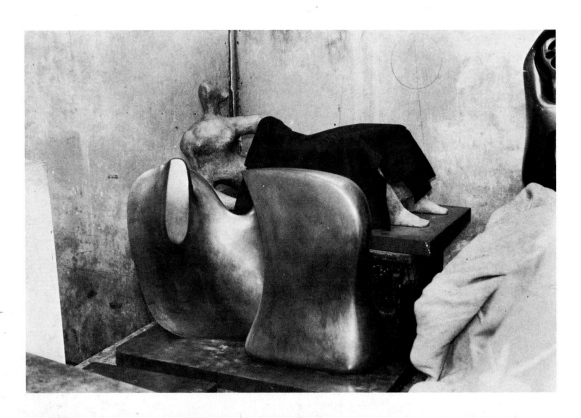

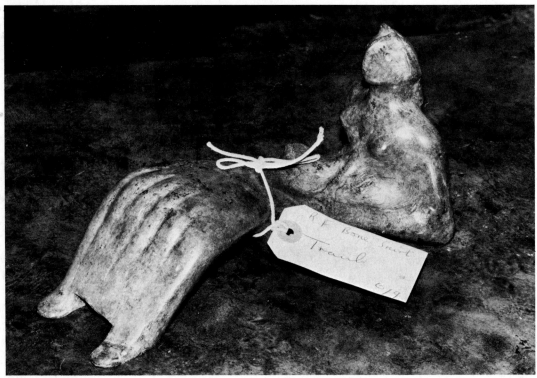

The White Studio with a bronze cast of *Draped Reclining Figure* 1952/3

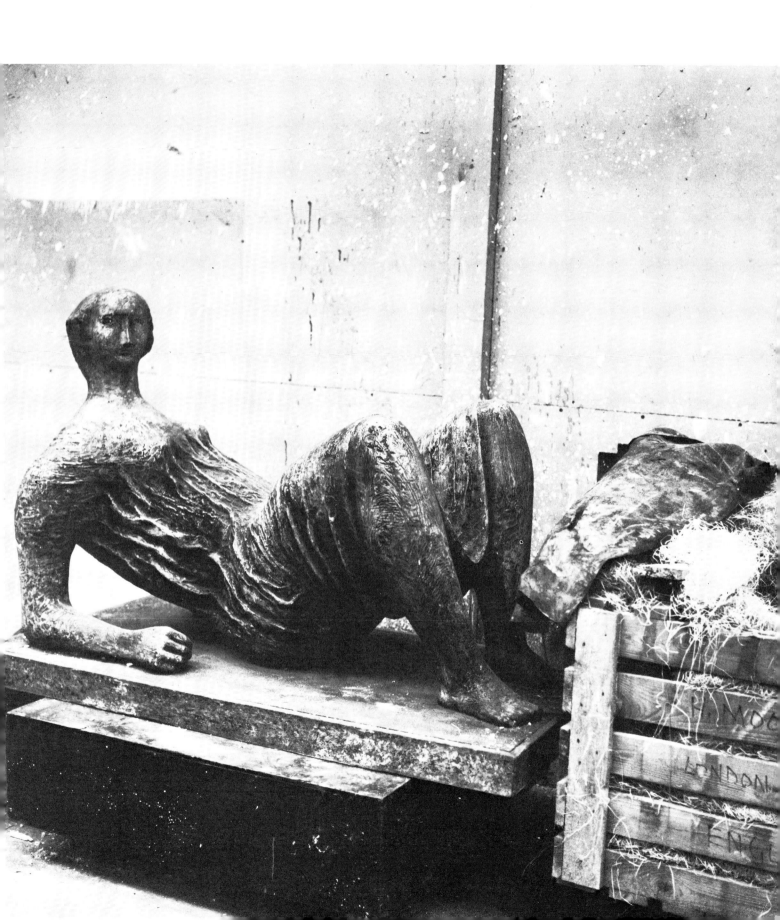

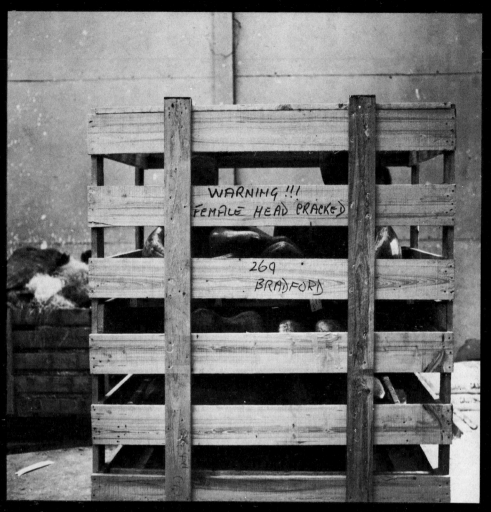

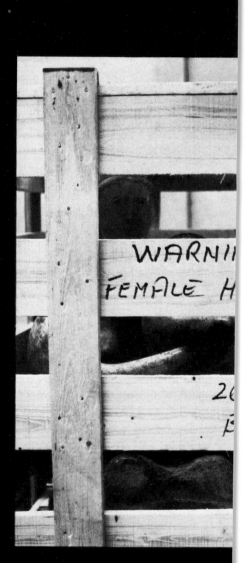

Ready for transportation to an exhibition in Bradford;
a plaster of *Family Group* 1948/9, crated with admonitions

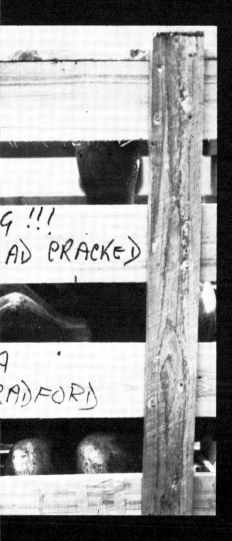

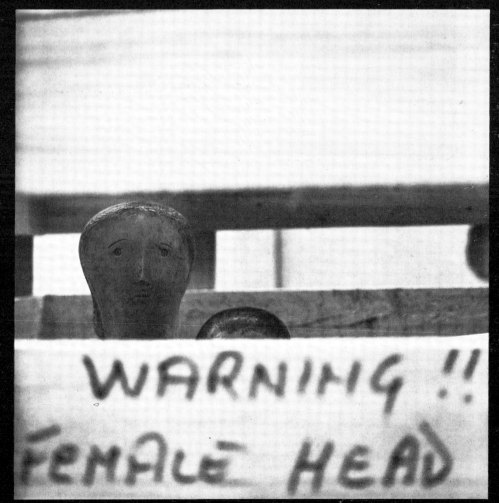

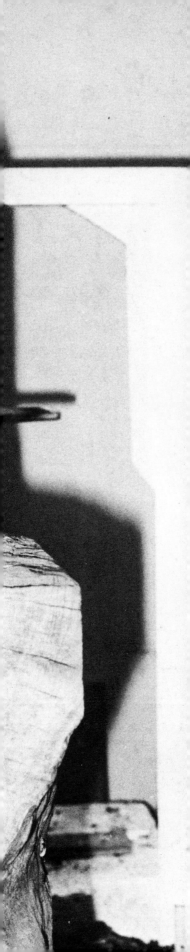

Progression of Ideas

The average sculpture is made in two opposite ways, either by building up in little bits, as one does with clay; or by taking something that is bigger than one wants and cutting it down to the required shape. Modelling is building up, carving is cutting down, whether the carving is in wood, stone, alabaster or soap. At college, we were not allowed to carve direct in stone. Instead we were taught the process of copying with a pointing machine, which is a method that was introduced and perfected after the Renaissance.

When I began doing sculpture, a few of the older sculptors like Brancusi, Modigliani and Epstein had begun to realise, through their admiration for primitive art, that those things that they had been admiring had all been made by direct carving. I arrived just at the period of this almost fanatical belief in making the sculpture by direct carving, and it was a wonderful thing. But gradually you find that these single-minded crusades always leave something out. So now I don't believe that direct carving in itself produces good sculpture; it doesn't. What produces good sculpture is a good mind. You don't make a good sculpture just by using a certain process, although it could help. I didn't like wood as a material to begin with, although some of my favourite carvings are in wood. Wood is a clean material that can be carved indoors. When I was a student, I could carve wood in my digs in Chelsea, but I couldn't carve stone in digs. Wood is also softer and easier to carve when first cut down. It hardens with time.

In 1975, Henry Moore was given the trunk of a large elm tree. His last *Reclining Figure* in wood had been completed in 1964. He started carving the new figure in the early summer of 1976 and the sculpture was completed two years later. The sequence of photographs shows the work in progress over the two-year period

Left: Malcolm Woodward, one of Henry Moore's assistants, starting work on *Reclining Figure: Holes*

Right: Henry Moore and Malcolm Woodward
discussing the plaster maquette for the new
elmwood sculpture

Left and below: 16 January 1978

Following pages: 26 January 1978

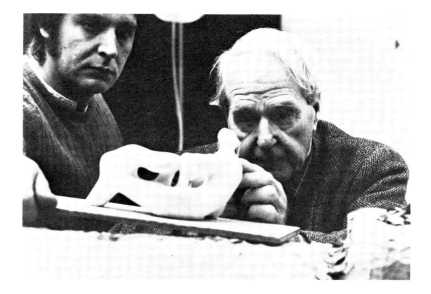

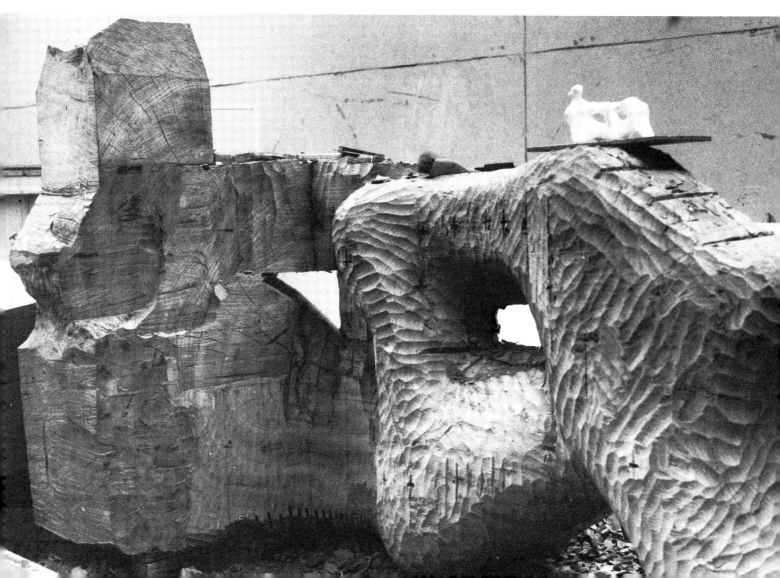

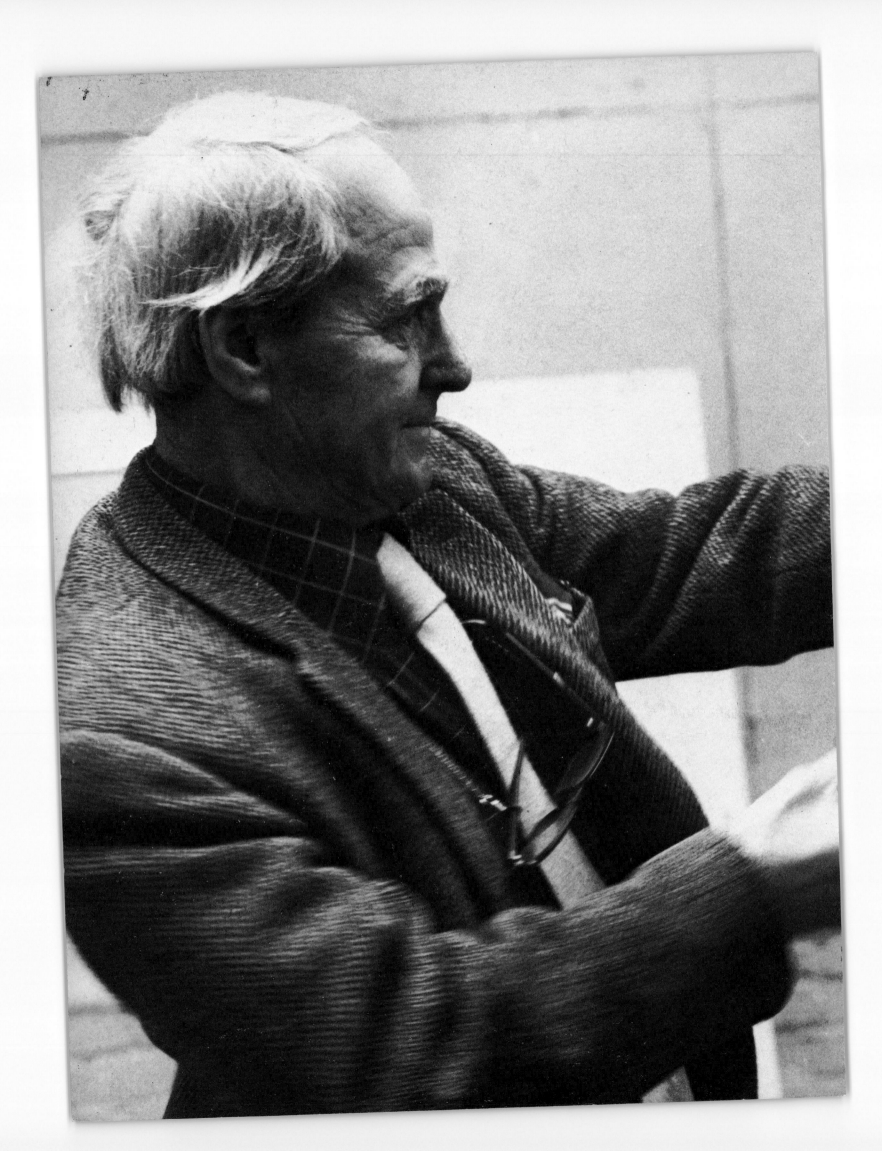

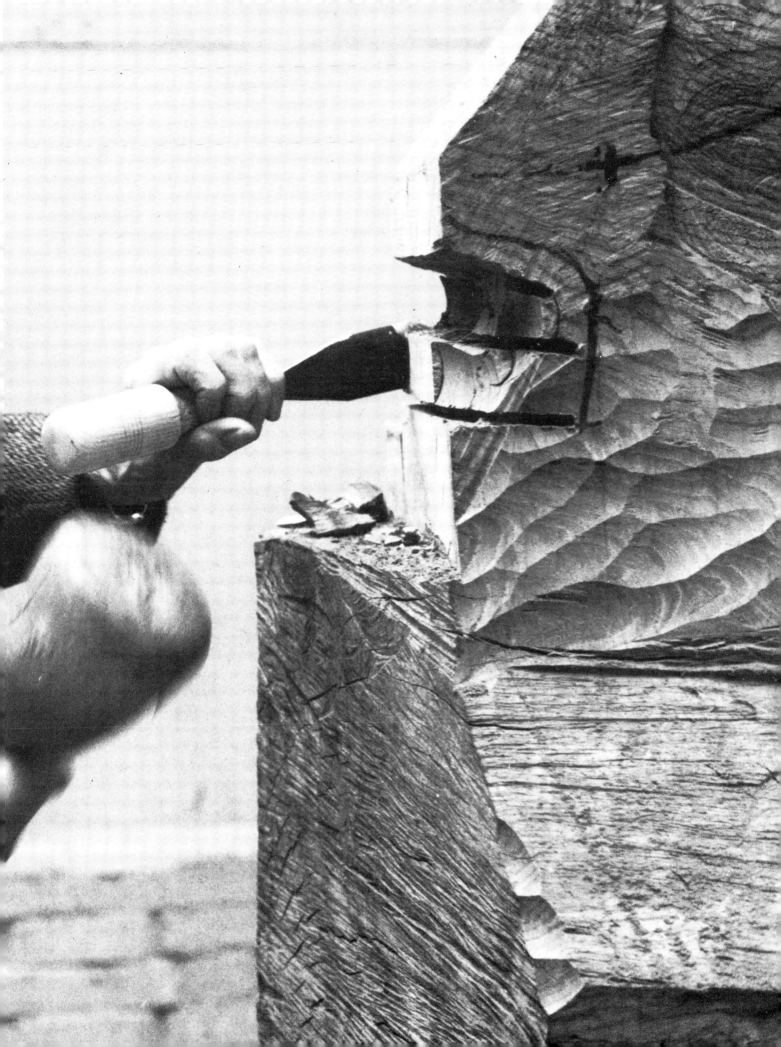

26 January 1978

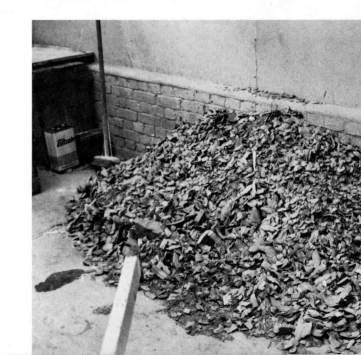

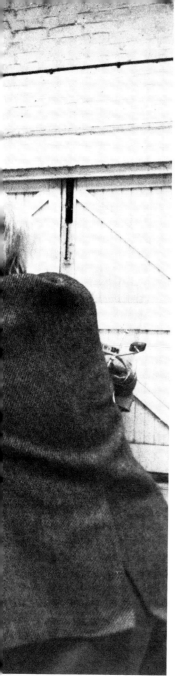

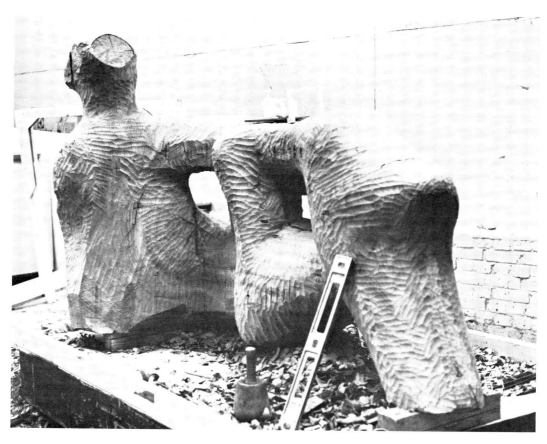

15 March 1978

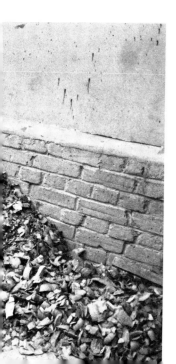

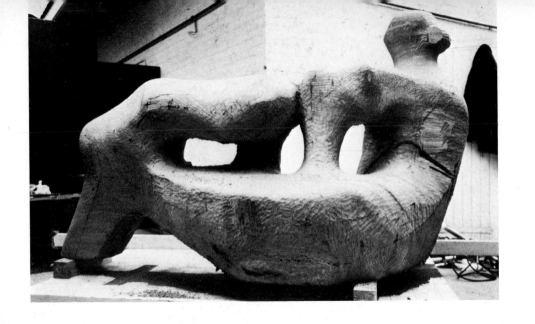

Henry Moore with various assistants turning over the sculpture so that it could be worked on underneath: 15 March 1978

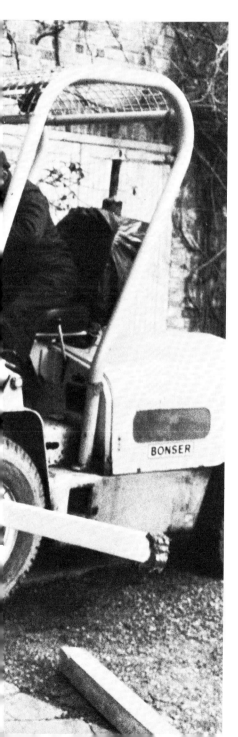

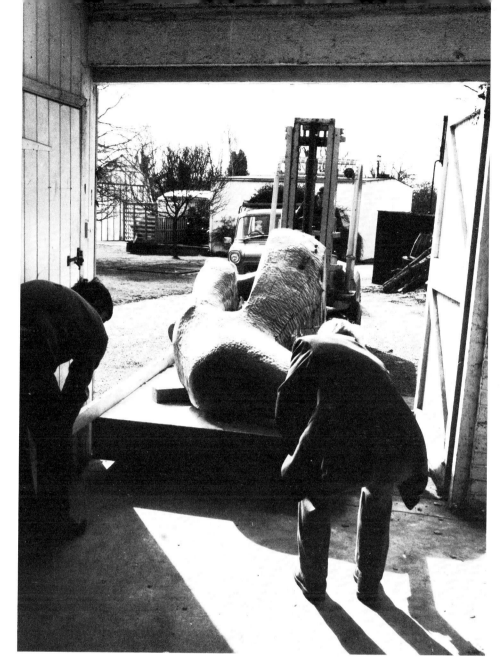

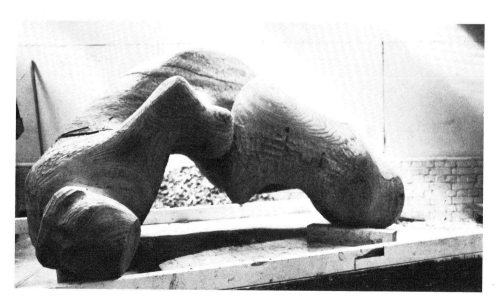

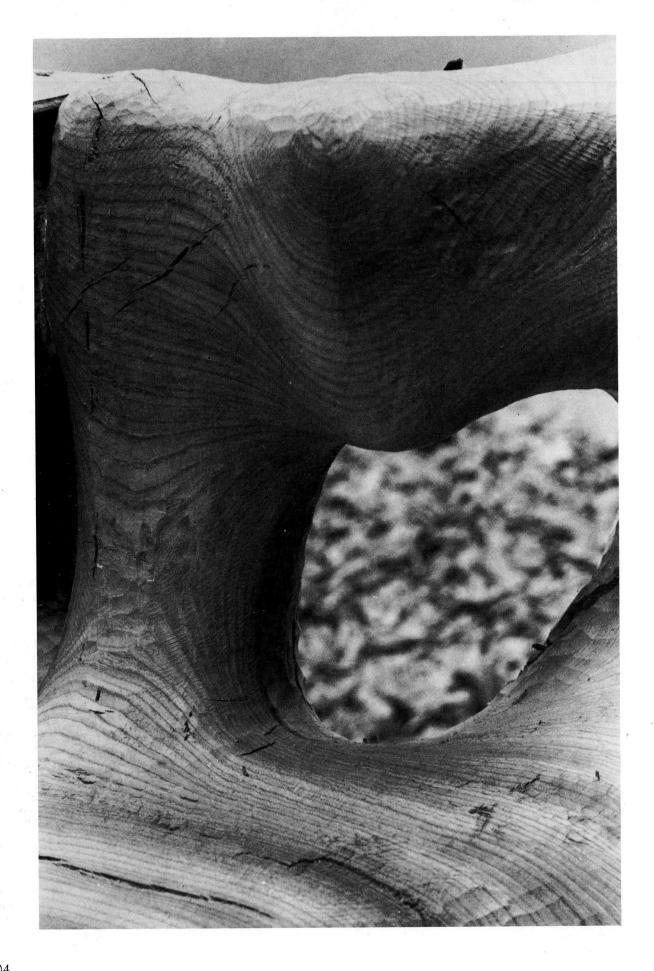

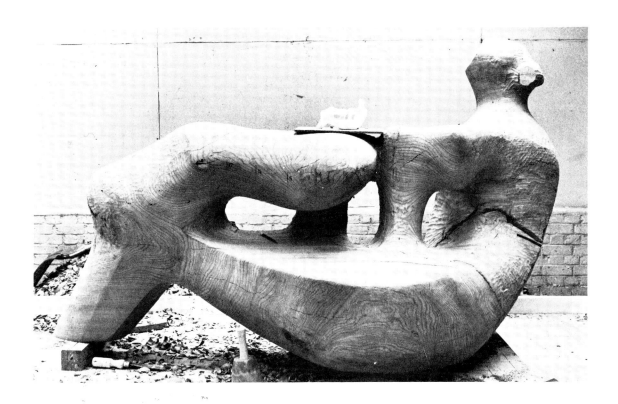

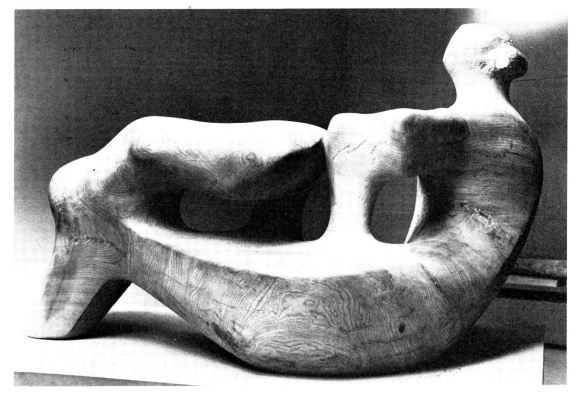

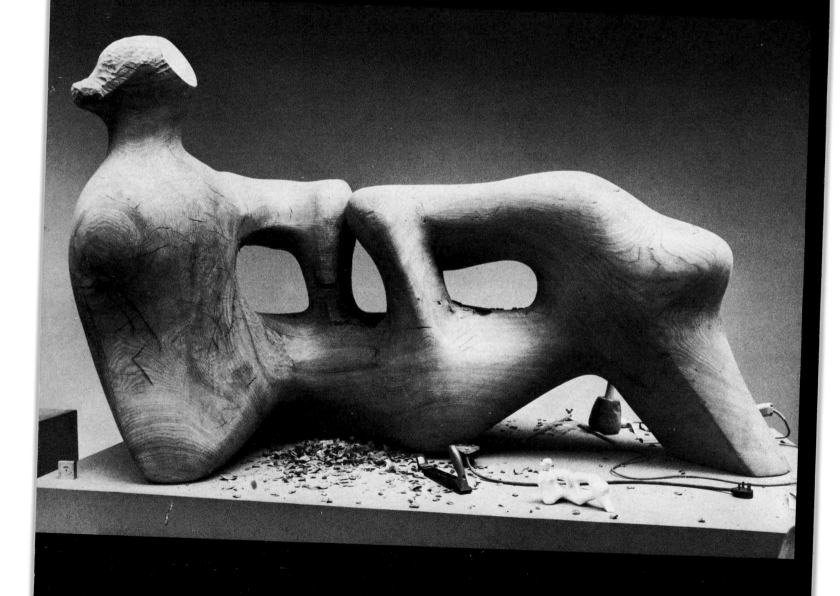

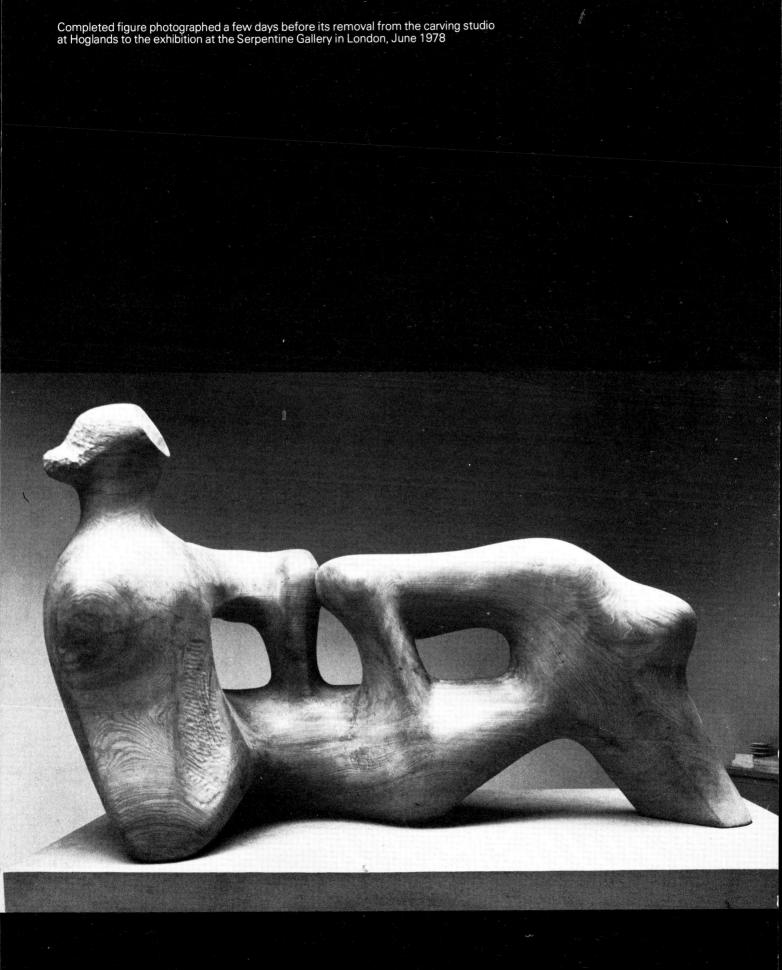

Completed figure photographed a few days before its removal from the carving studio
at Hoglands to the exhibition at the Serpentine Gallery in London, June 1978

I have taken my own photographs for sculpture since about 1925. When I was no longer a student, photographs began to be necessary – one would exhibit, and photographs were asked for. To begin with, I employed a photographer from Hammersmith who mainly took portraits and wedding photographs. I had a studio in Hammersmith, and some of the very early photographs are of that studio, taken by the photographer. But I had to show him what view I wanted, or what light was best. He would charge me 7s.6d. and all he had done was to press the trigger, because I had set it all up. One day

I showed him a photograph by Brancusi to show him it was the shape of the sculpture that we were trying to get, not the background. He looked at it, saw the name, and said, 'Brancusi, a well known photographer!' Brancusi took all the photographs of his own sculpture and didn't allow anyone else to take them.

I asked the photographer what sort of camera was best and cheap, and I got one for about £9. From then on, I began to take all my own photographs, unless I wanted one of myself with a sculpture.

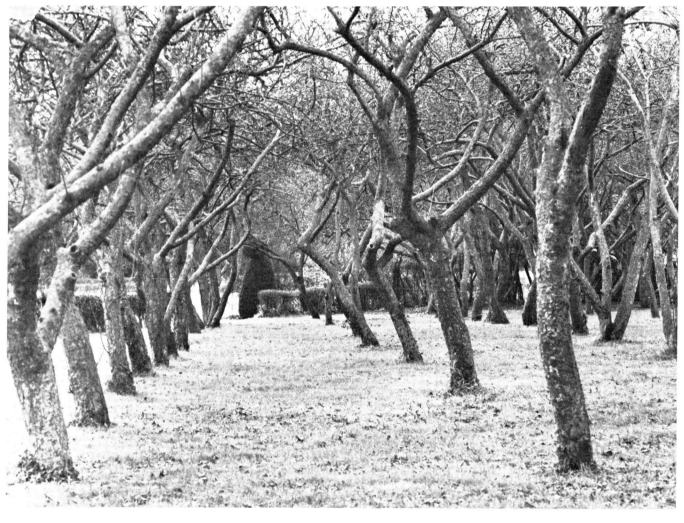

Above: Dane Tree House orchard in winter and (opposite) Henry Moore with his camera photographing the trees in the orchard. The photographs will provide him with references for his drawings and etchings

109

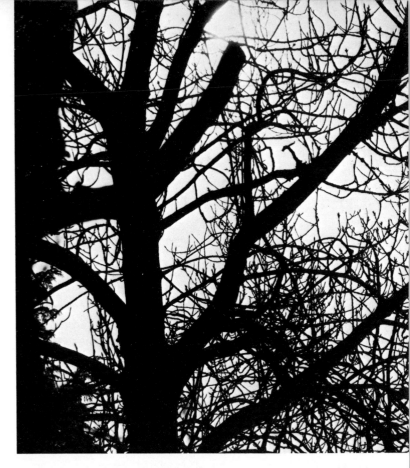

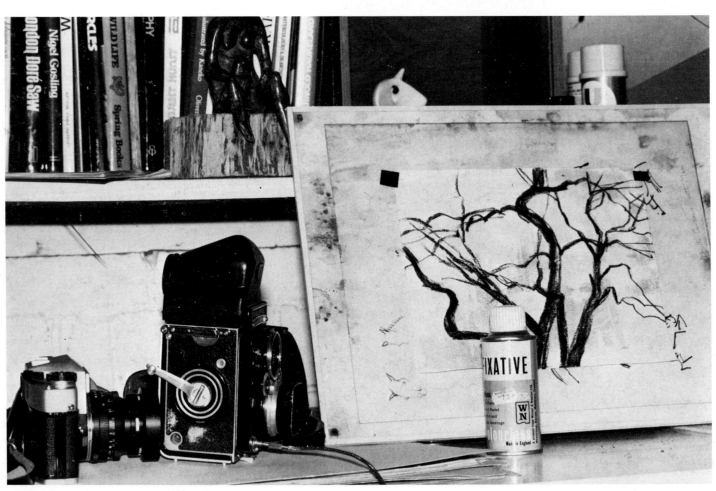

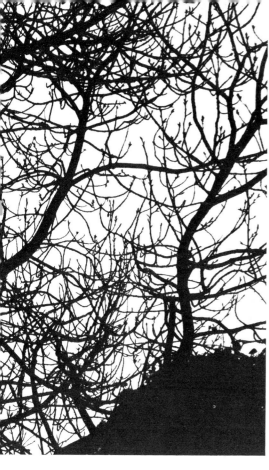

Left below: Charcoal drawing of branches

Below: Two finished drawings of the trees in the Gildmore graphic studio with, above, two states of new *Reclining Figure* etchings (see pages 120 & 121)

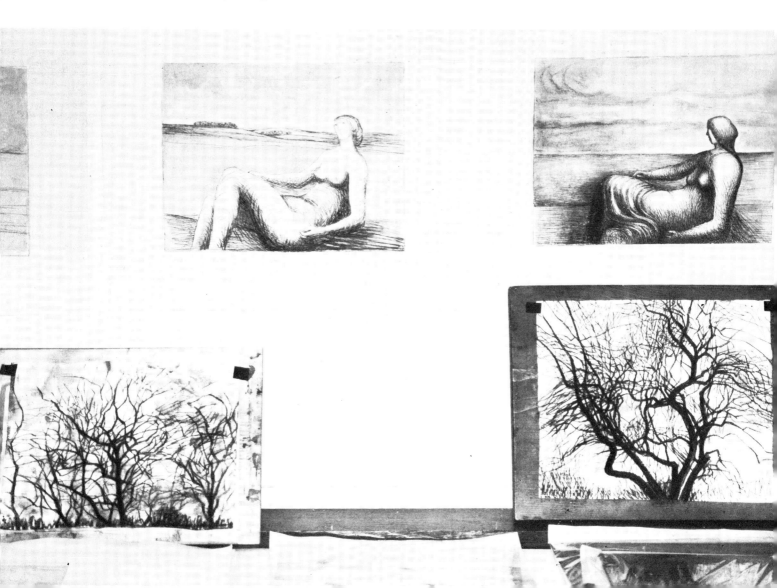

Tools

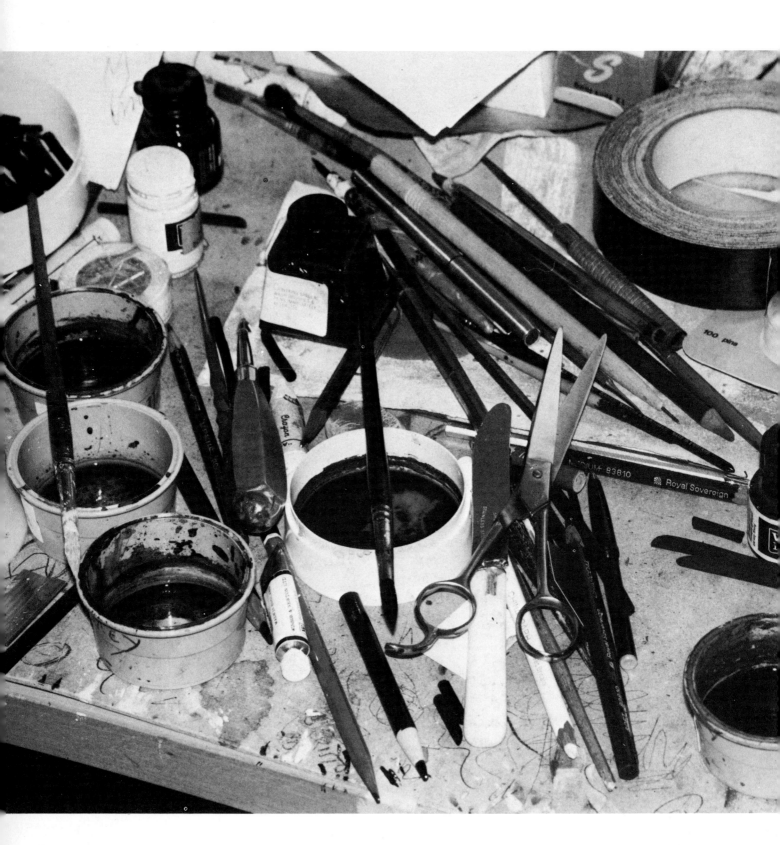

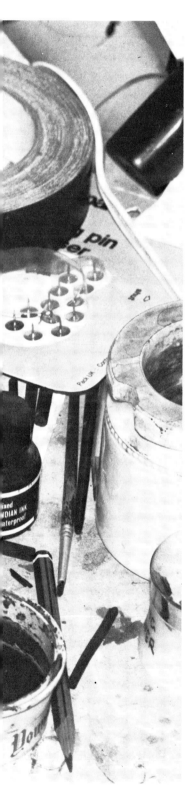

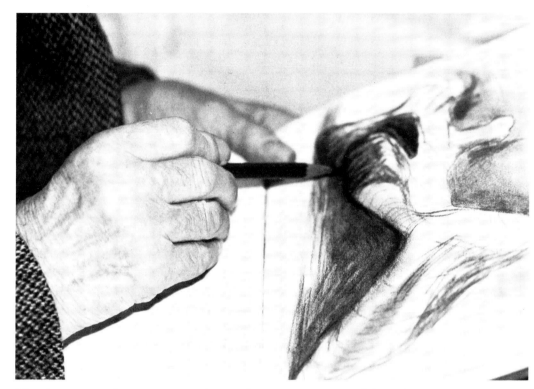

Tools are only an extension of your arms and hands.

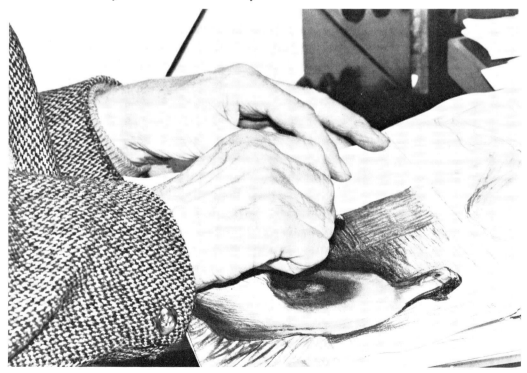

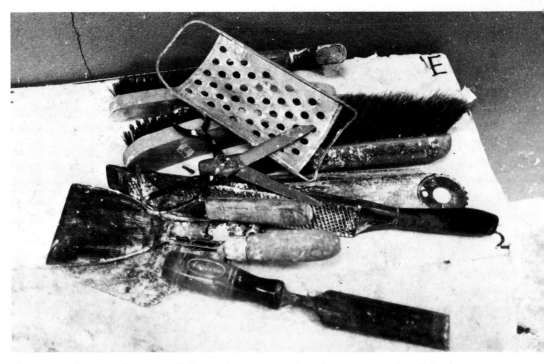

Any tools can be used for plasterwork, for example, kitchen tools such as cheese graters or nutmeg graters, spatulas, knives, or anything.

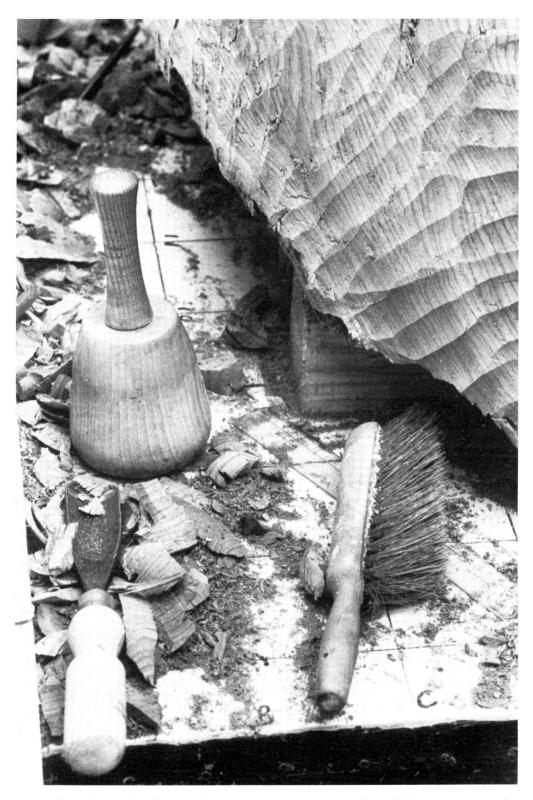

Woodcarving has to have a gouge, a curved tool, because wood has a fibrous grain. A flat tool could bury itself and split the wood instead of cutting it. So you have a gouge so that the two corners clear the wood and the cutting is done by the middle, curved part of the tool.

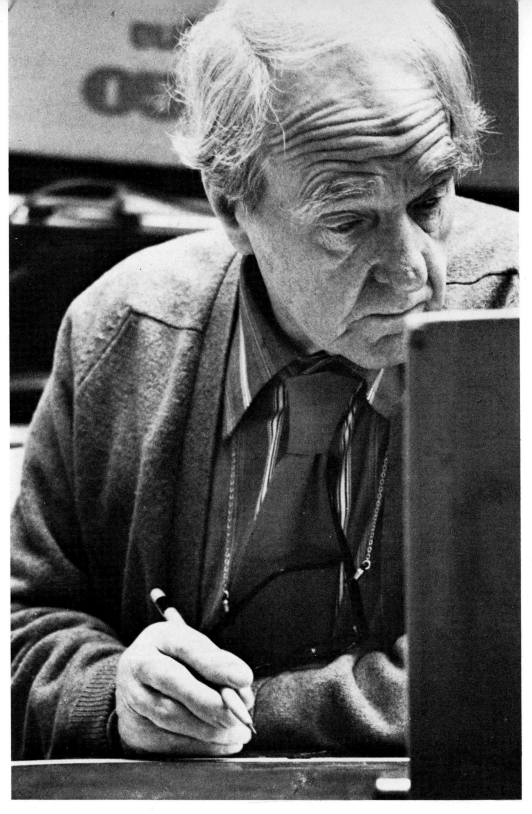

In the past few years, I have done much more graphic work than I used to, and for etching and lithography I must have all the tools around me. I have adapted a small studio and had a printing press put into it, where I do my etching. Etching has to be separated from lithography or ordinary drawing because dangerous acid is used in the process.

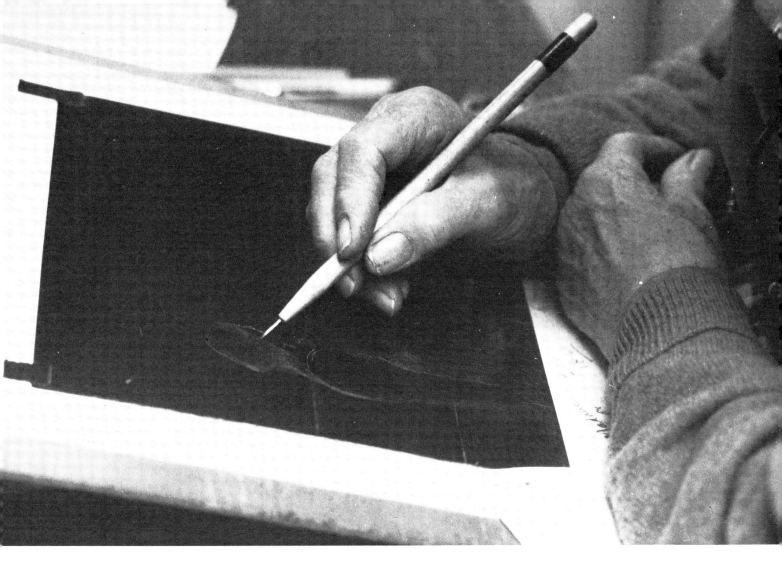

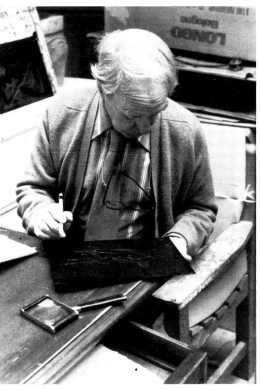

In etching, the copper plate is covered with a thin coating, a form of Shellac, which is resistant to acid. Where this coating is taken away by an etching needle or scraper, the acid bites into the exposed copper which then prints as a line or tone.

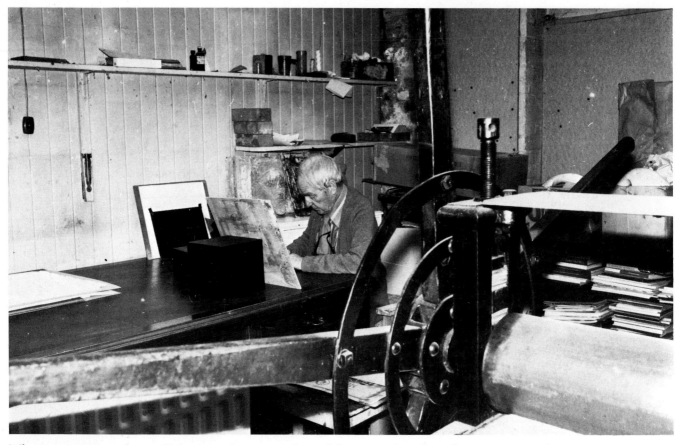

The majority of my lithographs are printed in London by the Curwen Press.

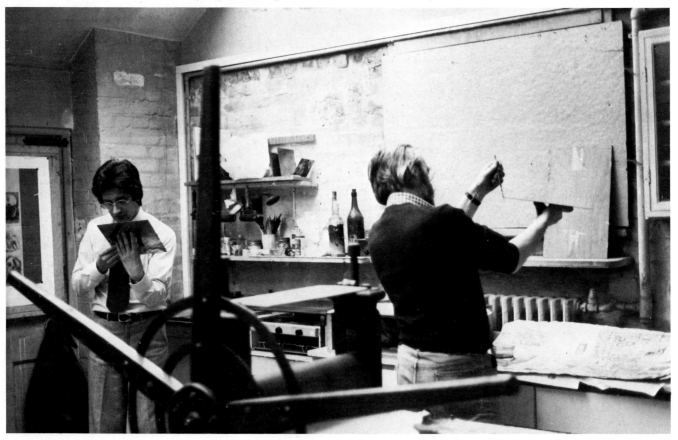

Top: Henry Moore at work on an etching in the etching studio with, in the foreground, the press that was installed in 1970
Above: David Mitchinson, on the left, examining the etching plate for any scratches in the varnish, and
Alistair Grant, on the right, 'stopping' the back and edges of the plate to protect it from the acid

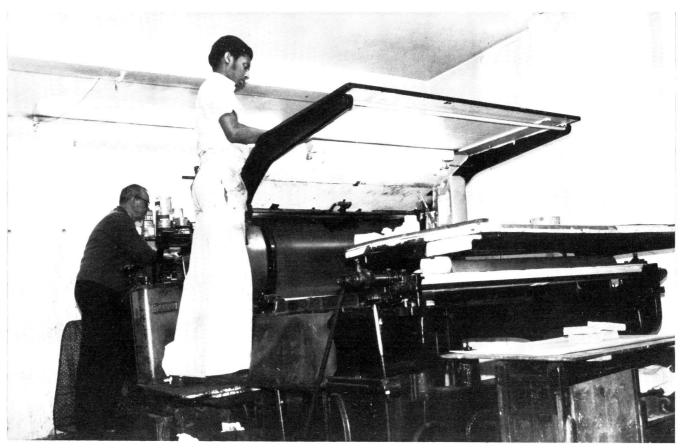

At the Curwen Press in London, preparing the print of one of the colours
for Henry Moore's lithograph, *Reclining Figure Interior Setting I*

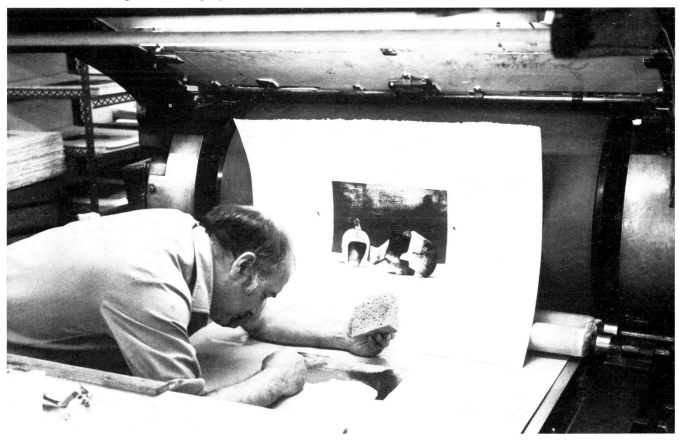

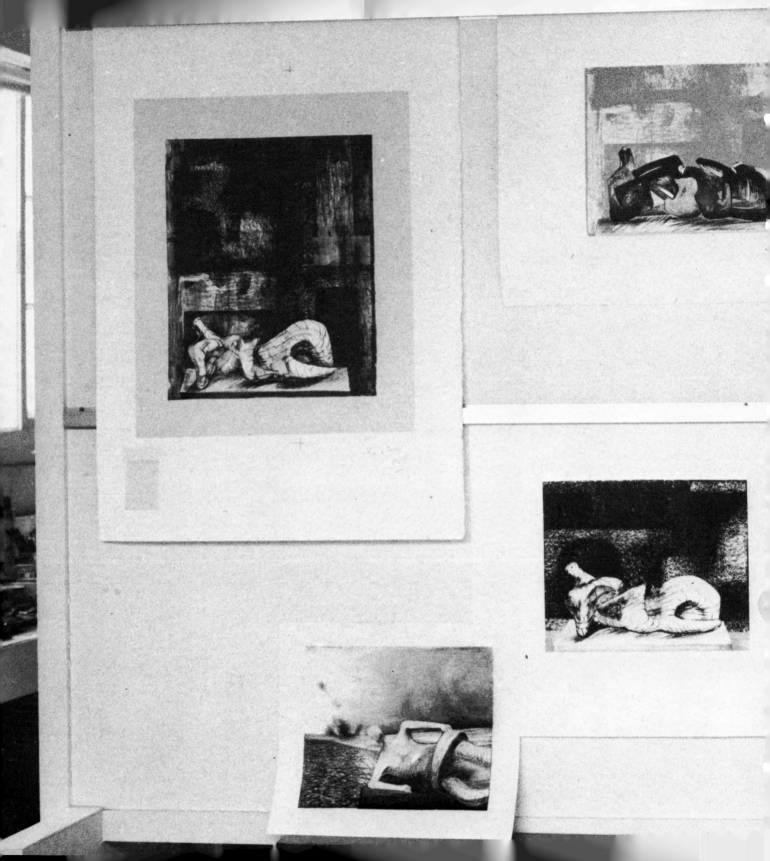

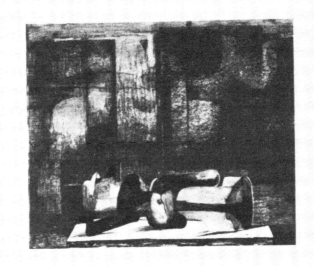

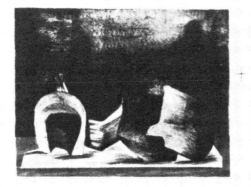

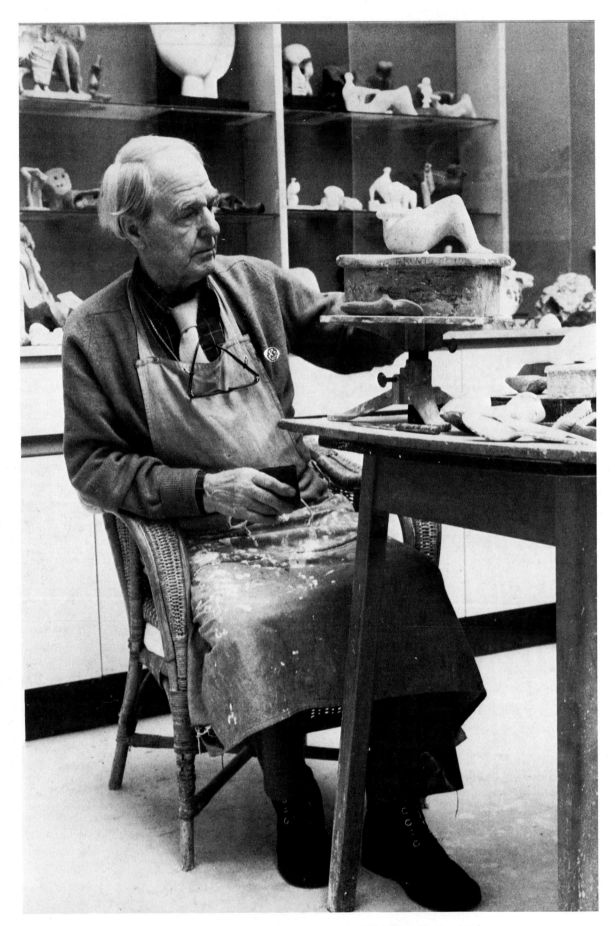

Henry Moore in his maquette studio, studying a plaster maquette of *Reclining Figure: Angles*

Execution of Work

For the past twenty years or more, I have gradually changed from using preliminary drawings for my sculptures to working from the beginning in three dimensions. That is, I first make a maquette for any idea that I have for a sculpture. The maquette is only three or four inches in size, and I can hold it in my hand, turning it over to look at it from above, underneath, and in fact from every angle. Thus, from the very beginning I am working and thinking in three dimensions.

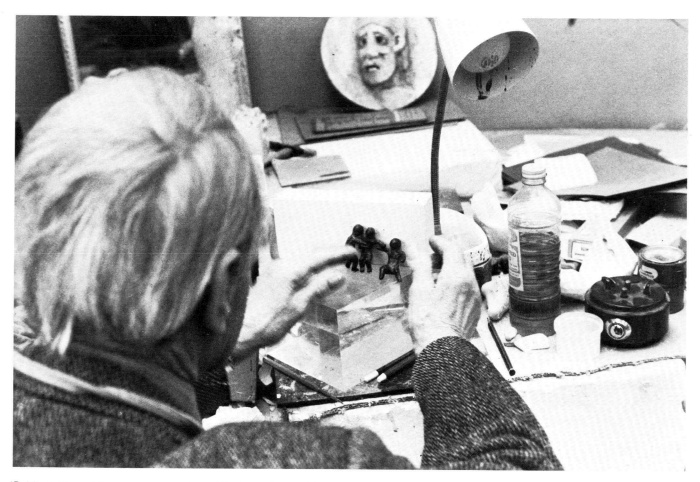

'Babies': Henry Moore experimenting with alternative positions for figures on base, in the Gildmore maquette studio

Plaster is an important material for sculptors. Good quality plaster mixed with water sets to the hardness of a soft stone. I use plaster for my maquettes in preference to clay because I can both build it up and cut it down. It is easily worked, while clay hardens and dries, so that it cannot be added to.

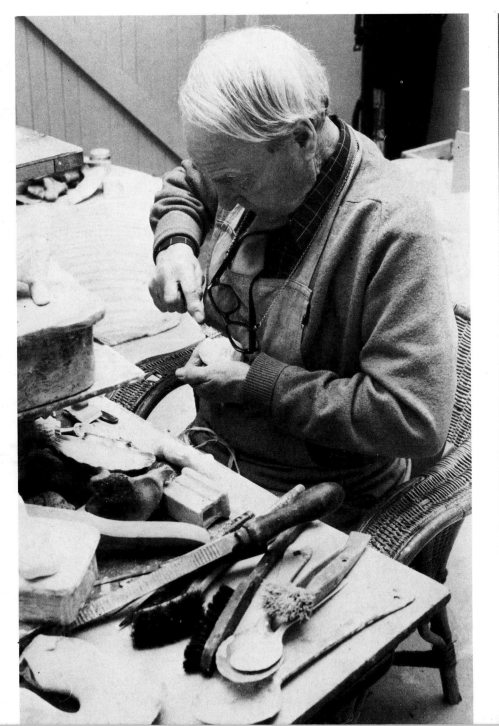

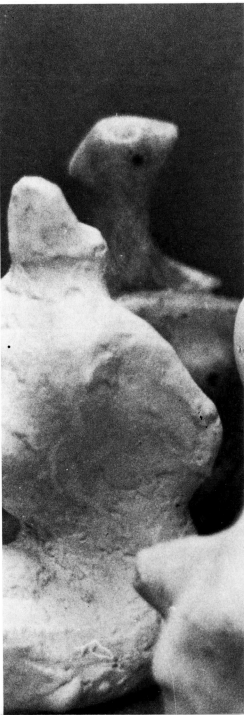

A miscellany of plaster maquettes

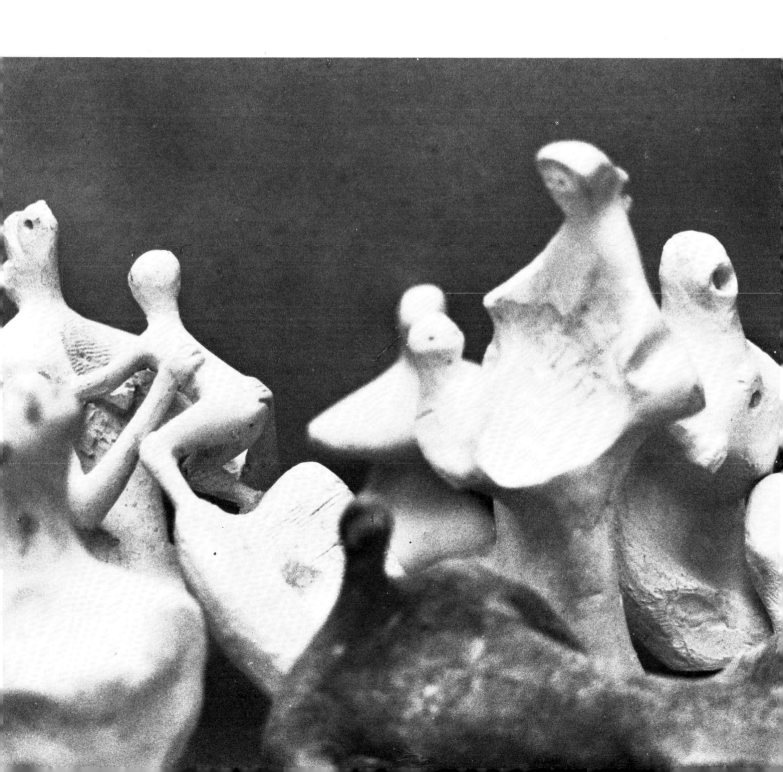

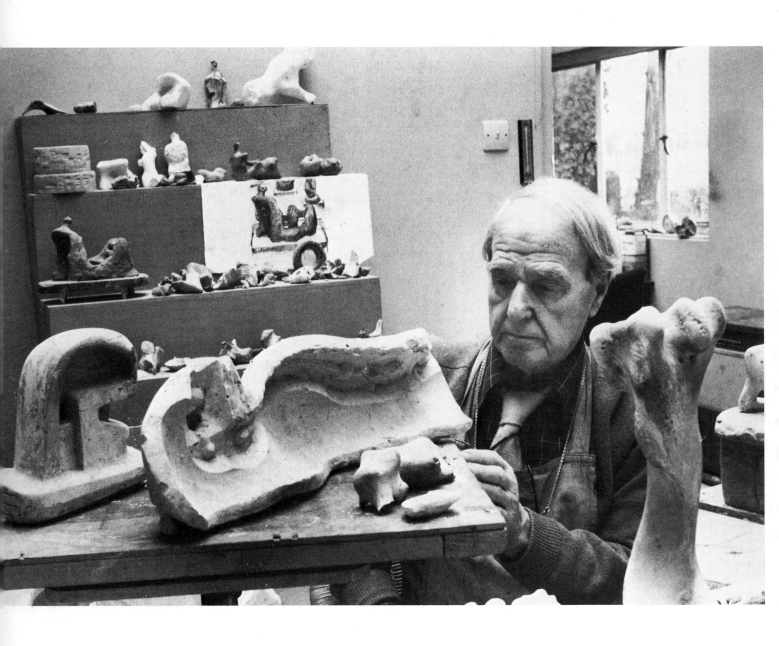

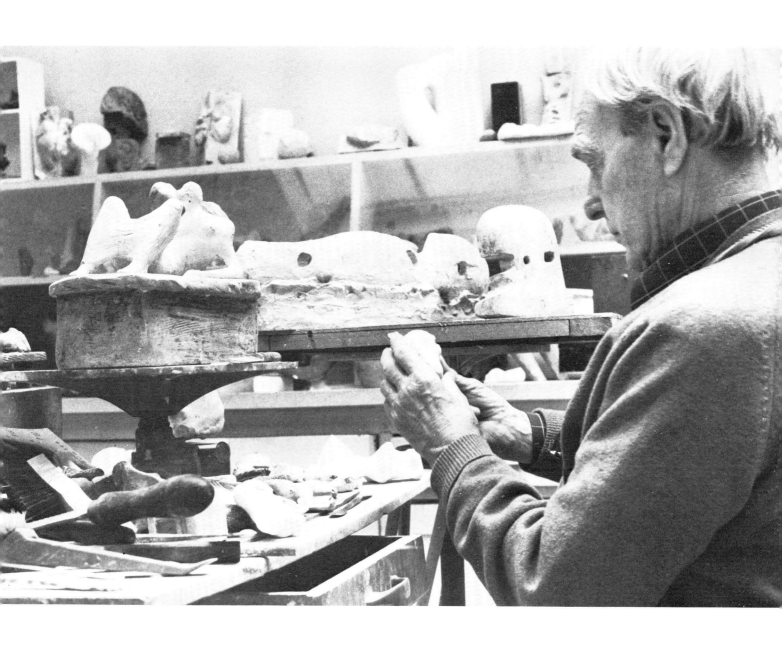

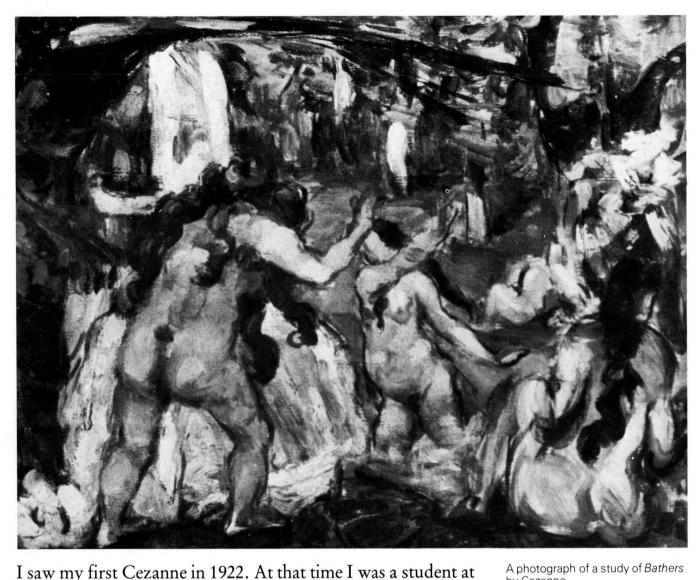

A photograph of a study of *Bathers* by Cezanne

I saw my first Cezanne in 1922. At that time I was a student at the Royal College of Art in London, and Raymond Coxon, a fellow student, and I were given permission to go to Paris during term-time. William Rothenstein, the principal of the college, asked us why we wanted to go. We said we wanted to see contemporary paintings, but in particular we both wanted to see the works of Cezanne. Rothenstein said that he would give us an introduction to M. Pellerin, who owned several Cezannes. At that time, many people thought that Cezanne was a 'trier', but not naturally gifted – not like Manet. We went to M. Pellerin's house and when we were admitted through the front door, there, directly in front of us, was the large *Women Bathers* (now in the Philadelphia Museum of Art). For me it was like seeing Chartres Cathedral – the visual experience was just as great.

128

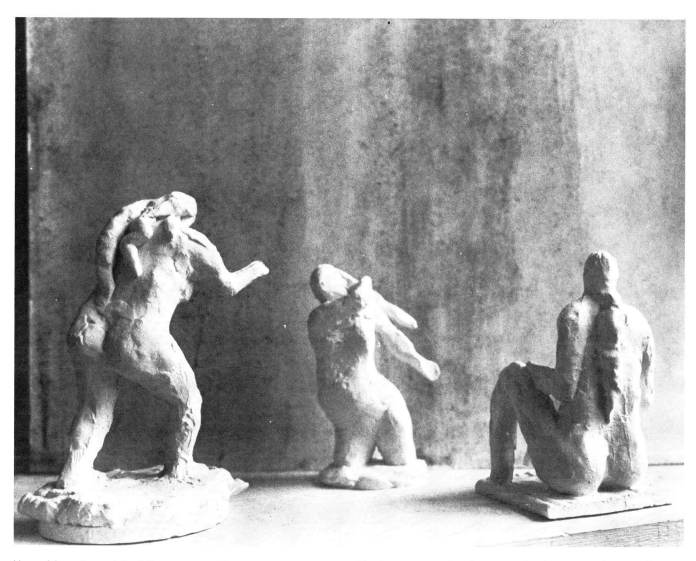

Henry Moore's models of figures
from the *Bathers*

I now own a small Cezanne *Bathers* painting, and in talking about it to friends, I have often said, 'look what a romantic idea Cezanne had of women,' and, 'how fully he realized the three-dimensional world'. I felt that I could easily make sculptures of his figures.

Stephen Spender in a letter to me said, 'your idea of showing that you could make sculptures of the Cezanne figures is fascinating. Why don't you do it?' Soon after his letter, I felt like proving it, and modelled each of the three figures in plasticine, taking about an hour in all. My idea was to show their existence completely in space, and perhaps to photograph them or make drawings, as it were, from behind the picture, showing them from all sides and demonstrating that they had been conceived by Cezanne in full three dimensions.

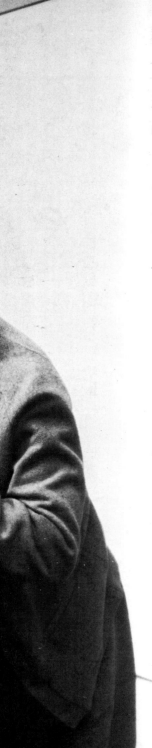

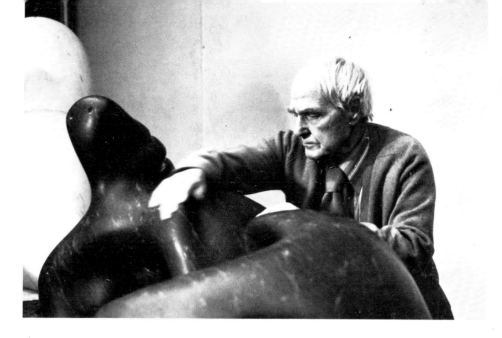

Henry Moore caressing areas of
Reclining Figure: Curved 1977, in
black marble

Carving is a straightforward process of having a hard material and knocking, carving or bursting pieces off. The tools we have now for stone carving begin with what is called a pitcher, or a boaster, with which whole corners can be broken off. All stones tend to have a direction in which they break most easily because of their grain formation. Next comes the punch, or point, and we burst the stone all round with the point when we hit it. That allows us to get large amounts off at a time. After that comes a claw tool, which is really a series of punches and points all in one instrument. When used on the stone, it leaves a series of parallel grooves. This was a favourite tool of Michaelangelo's. Next comes the chisel, which is flat.

Michaelangelo used his marble very soon after it was quarried, and this made what is a hard stone much quicker to carve. Michaelangelo was a very adept carver.

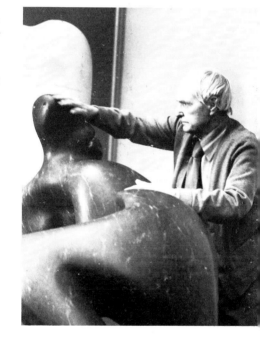

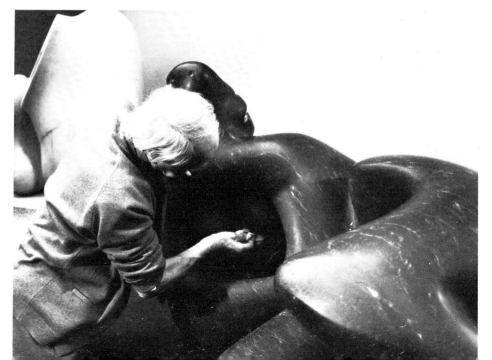

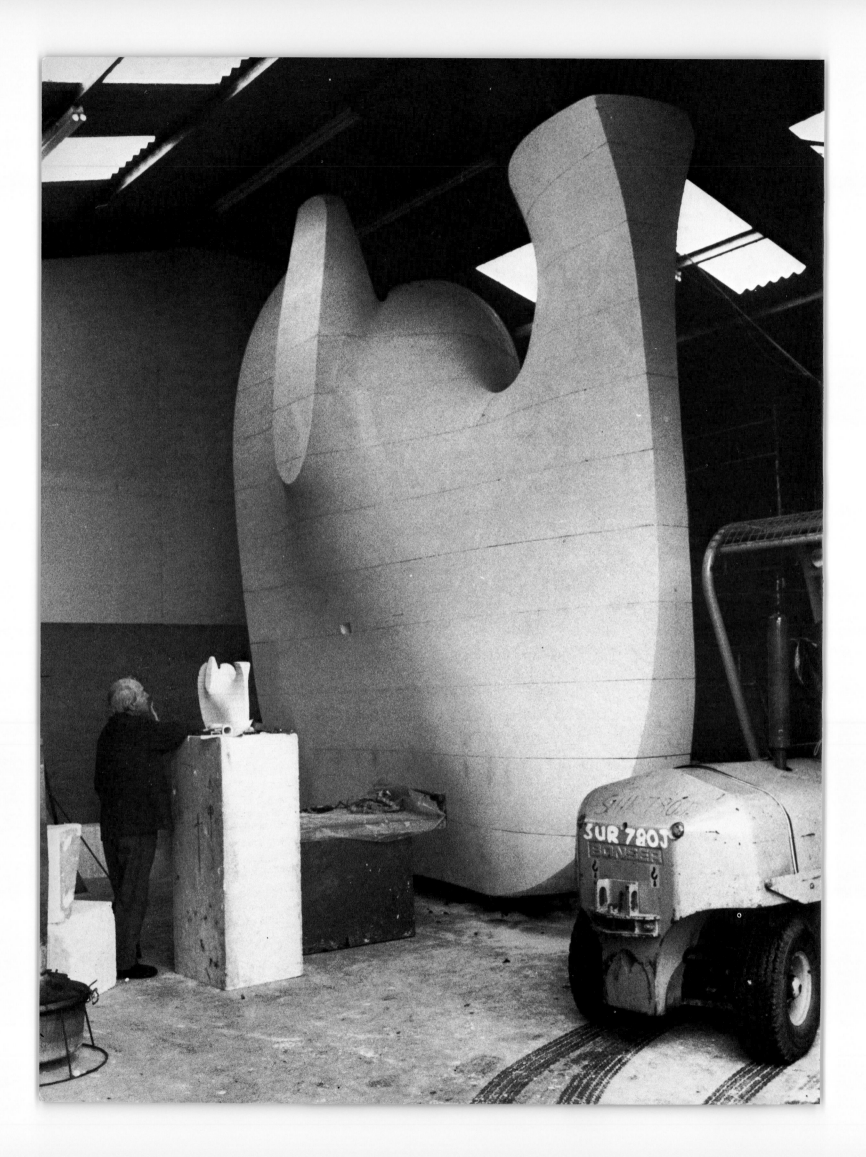

I first used polystyrene in the early 1960s, when I was asked to design the scenery for Mozart's opera *Don Giovanni.* Certain parts of the scenery were made in polystyrene. From then on, I realized that it was going to save a lot of time, energy and effort. The previous method had involved working with a wooden or metal armature, wire netting, canvas and plaster – which is heavy material in itself. This meant that, for example, a single form of the 'vertebrae' would need three of us to move it round. I can move polystyrene alone, the material is so light. That is its advantage; its disadvantage is that it is easily damaged.

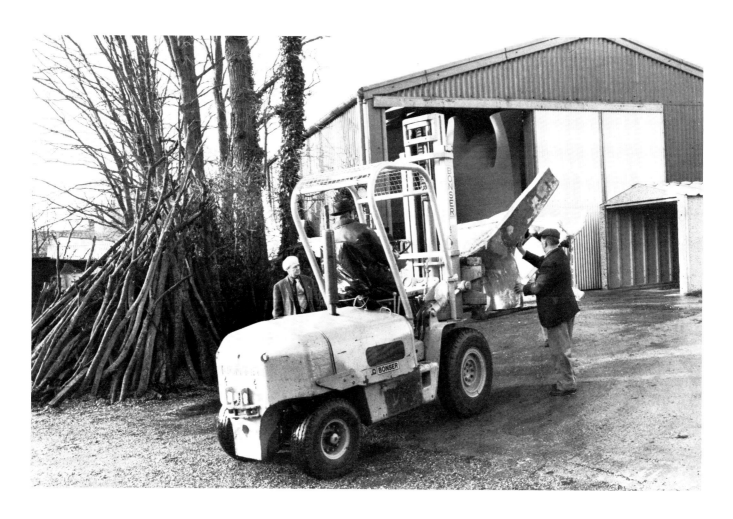

Most young sculptors cannot afford to have their work cast in bronze – I couldn't afford it until some time after the war. The work that I wanted cast into metal I would cast into lead, because I could melt lead on a kitchen gas ring. I ruined a lot of pans, but in 1939 and 1940 I made a lot of lead casts myself.

Bronze is difficult to cast yourself, because the higher melting point means you must have a furnace to melt the bronze. I have tried that in my garden at Much Hadham, but I had awful problems getting the bronze to melt. In fact, I was up pumping away with bellows trying to get it going till late at night.

Until recently, all my larger sculptures have been cast in West Berlin, in the Hermann Noack bronze foundry. In 1977, they were so occupied with work for a large exhibition that I was having in France, that they couldn't cope with the big sculpture that I was going to have cast for the National Gallery Extension in Washington.

If you have a sculpture with architecture, it needs to be very big. Modern architecture, with its height and massiveness, calls for a sculpture of a much bigger size than in previous times. Therefore I went to the Morris Singer foundry at Basingstoke to have the casting done. In fact, according to the bronze foundry, this is the biggest bronze that they think has ever been cast.

At the Morris Singer bronze foundry in Basingstoke, with the bronze cast of the other half of *Mirror Knife Edge* being prepared for the National Gallery Extension in Washington

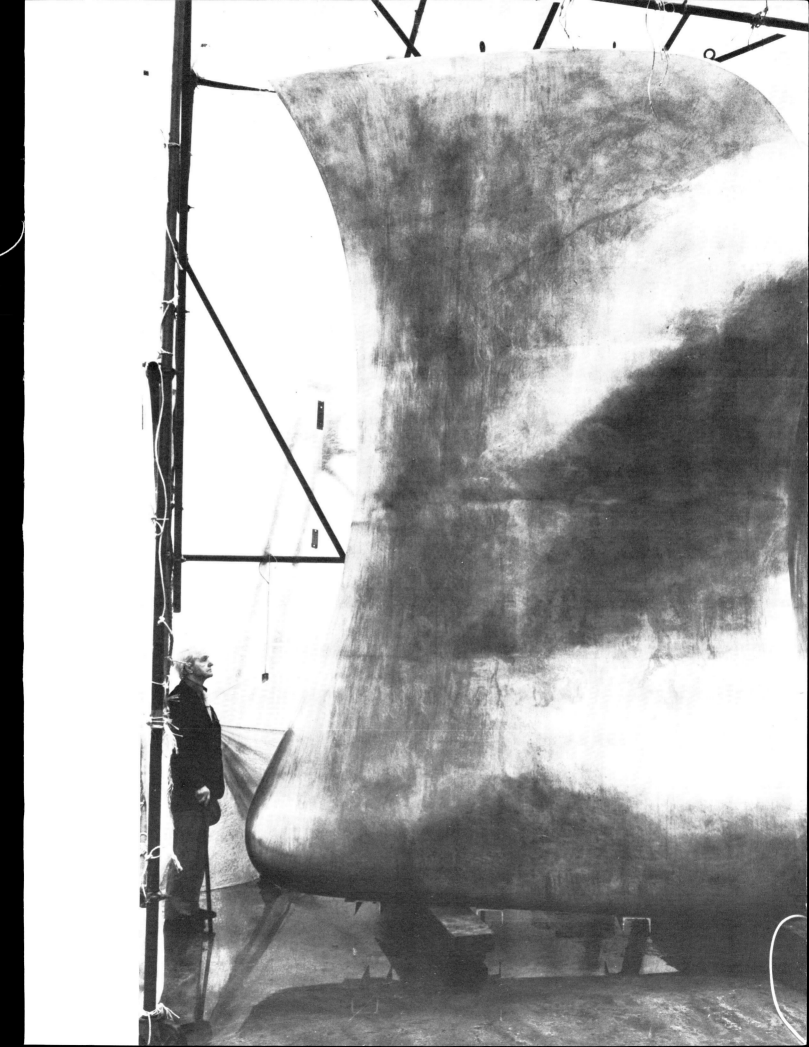

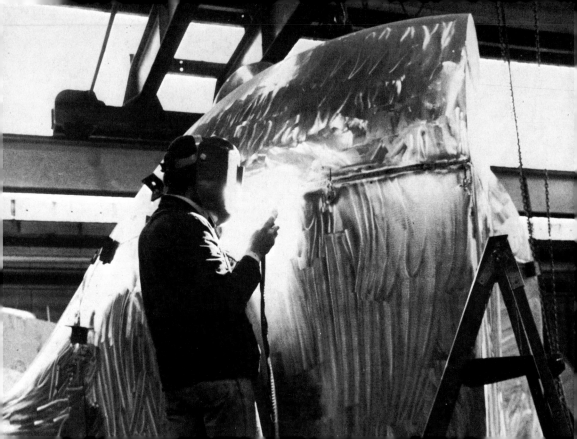

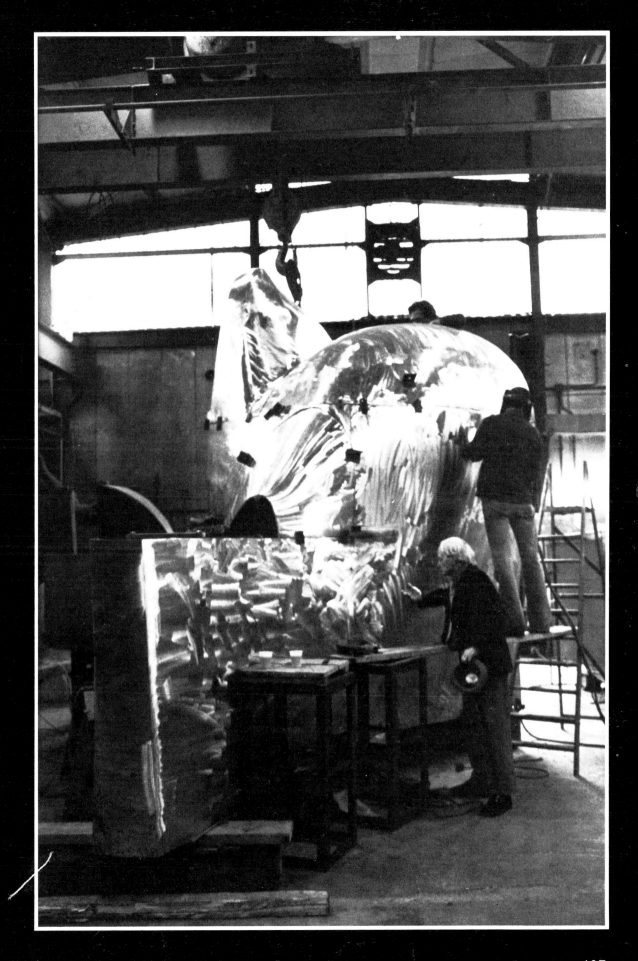

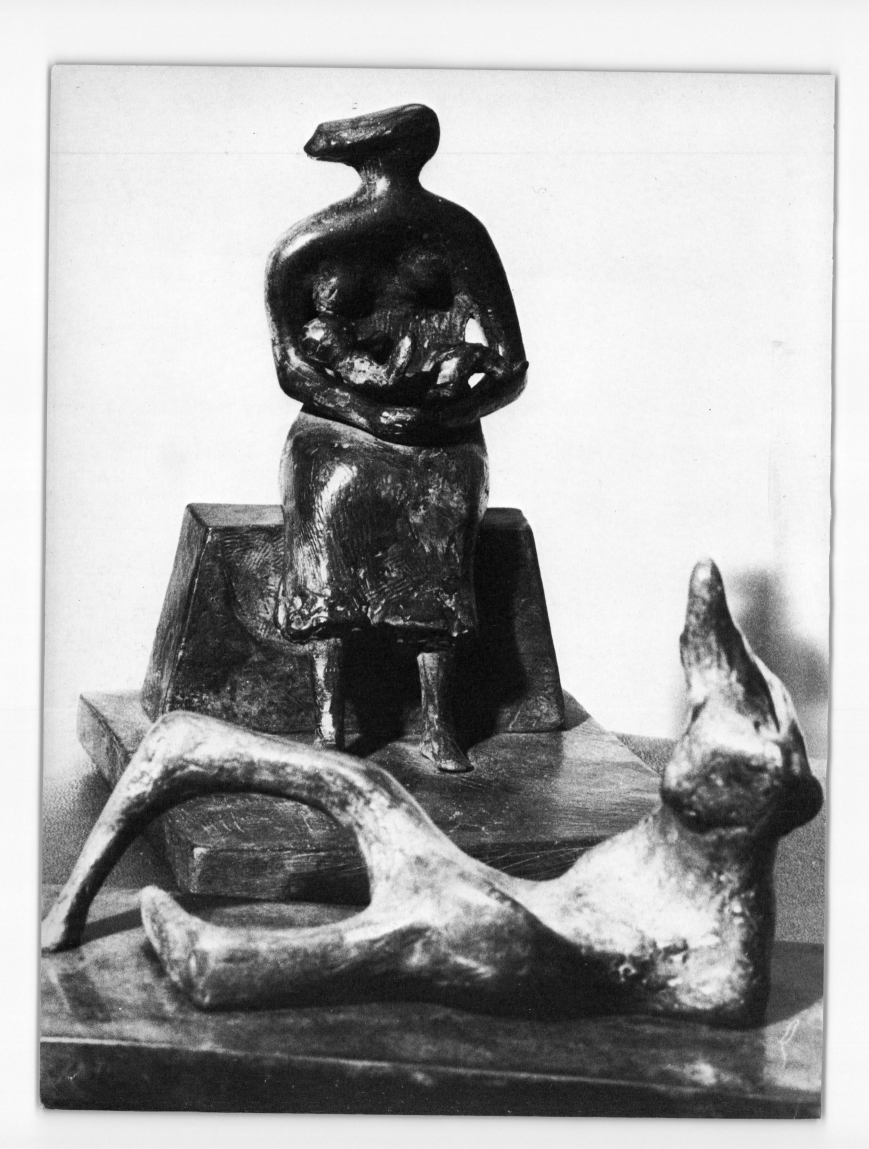

Finished Works

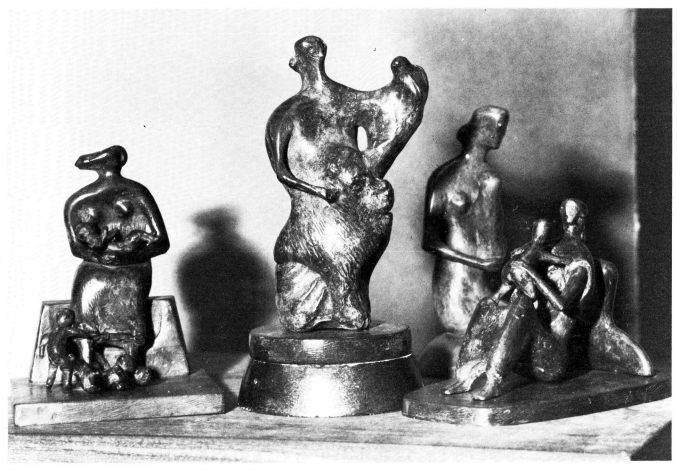

Left: *Mother and Child: Hair* 1977, and *Reclining Figure: Crossed Legs* 1976, both in bronze
Above: Group of small bronze maquettes

Below and right: *Reclining Figure: Curved* 1977, in black marble

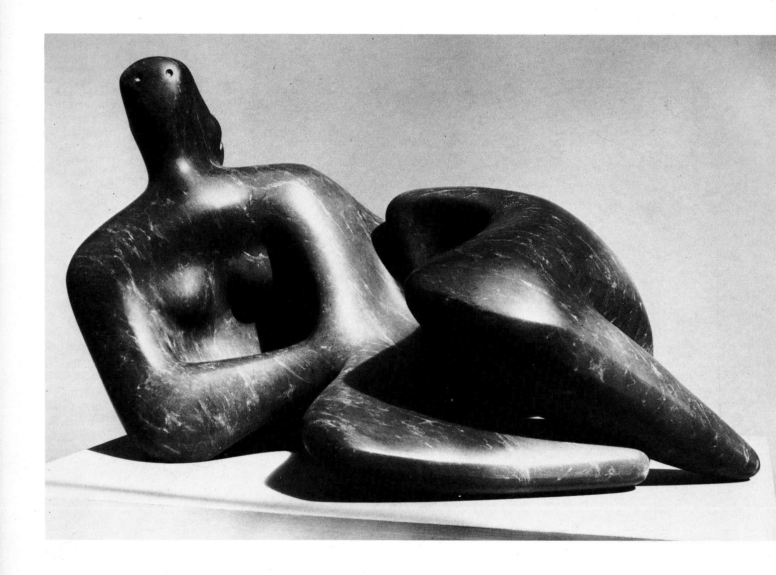

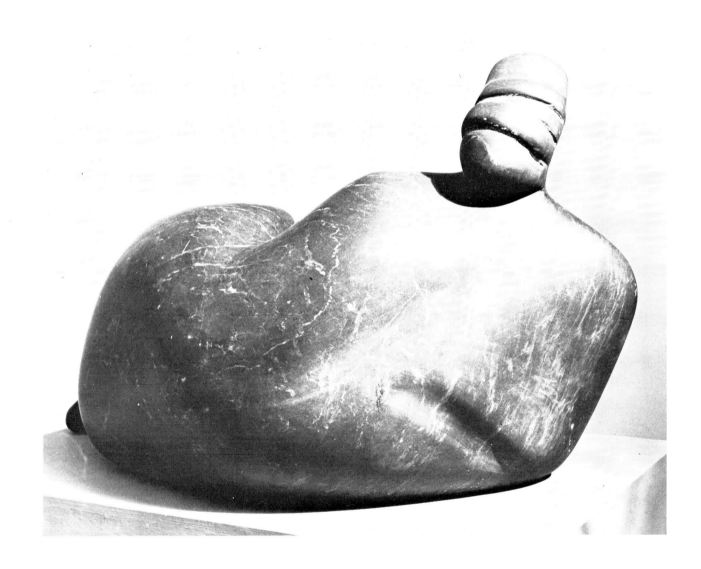

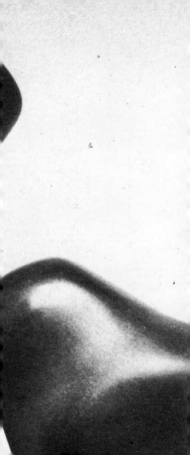

Granite is one of the hardest stones, it would last for thousands of years in any climate. Very few other stones will stay out of doors as well as bronze.

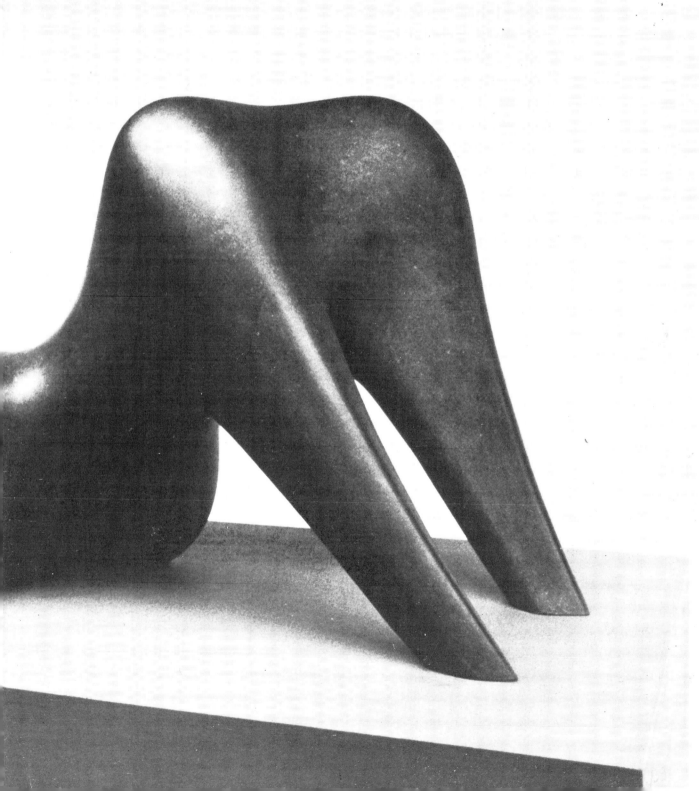

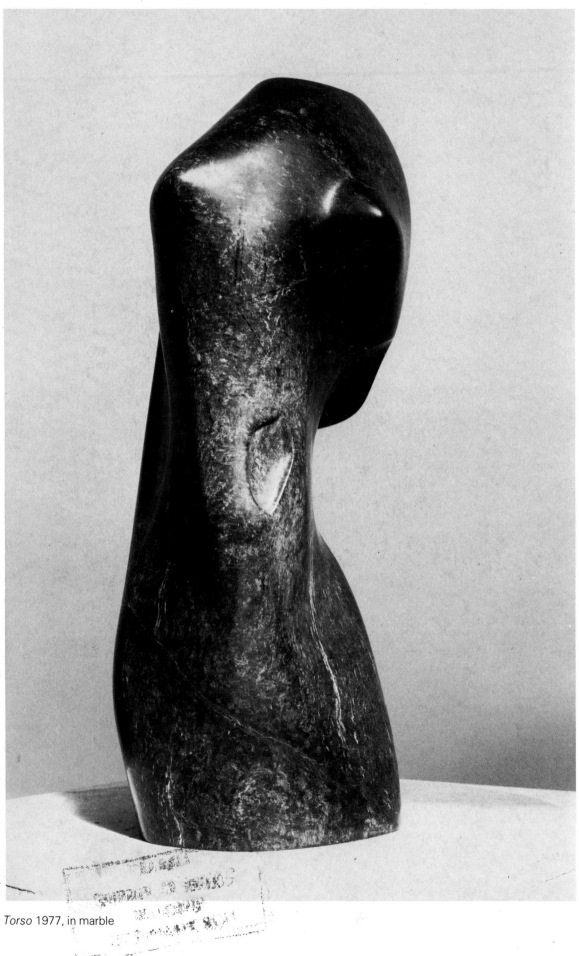

Torso 1977, in marble

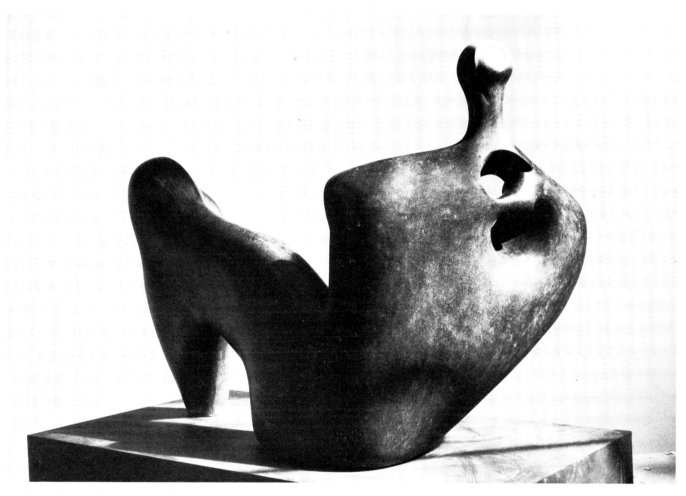

Reclining Figure: Single Leg 1976, in black granite

145

Below: *Two Piece Reclining Figure: Double Circle* 1976, in black marble

Opposite: *Mother and Child: Egg Form* 1977, in white marble

I now use many varieties of marble, but in the early part of my career I made a point of using native materials because I thought that, being English, I should understand our stones. They were cheaper, and I could go round to a stonemason and buy random pieces. I tried to use English stones that hadn't been used before for sculpture. I discovered many English stones, including Hornton Stone, from visiting the Geological Museum in South Kensington, which was next door to my college.

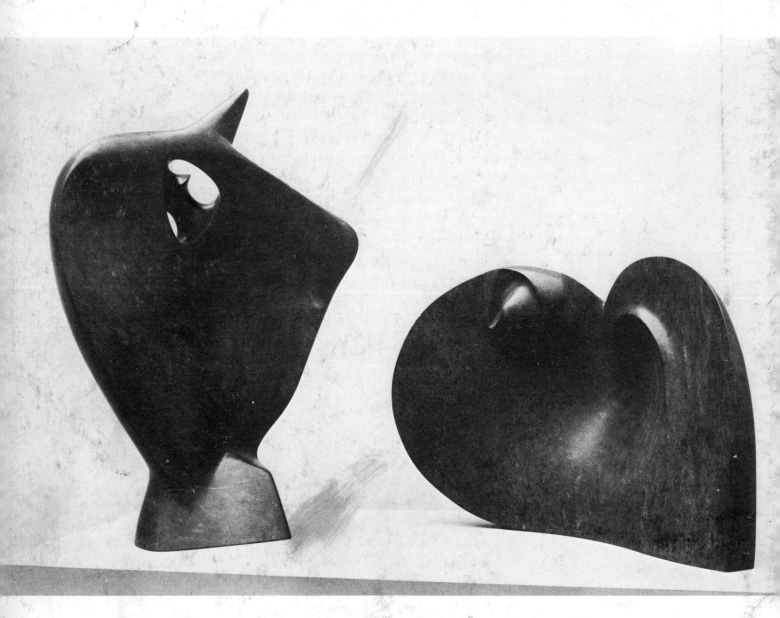

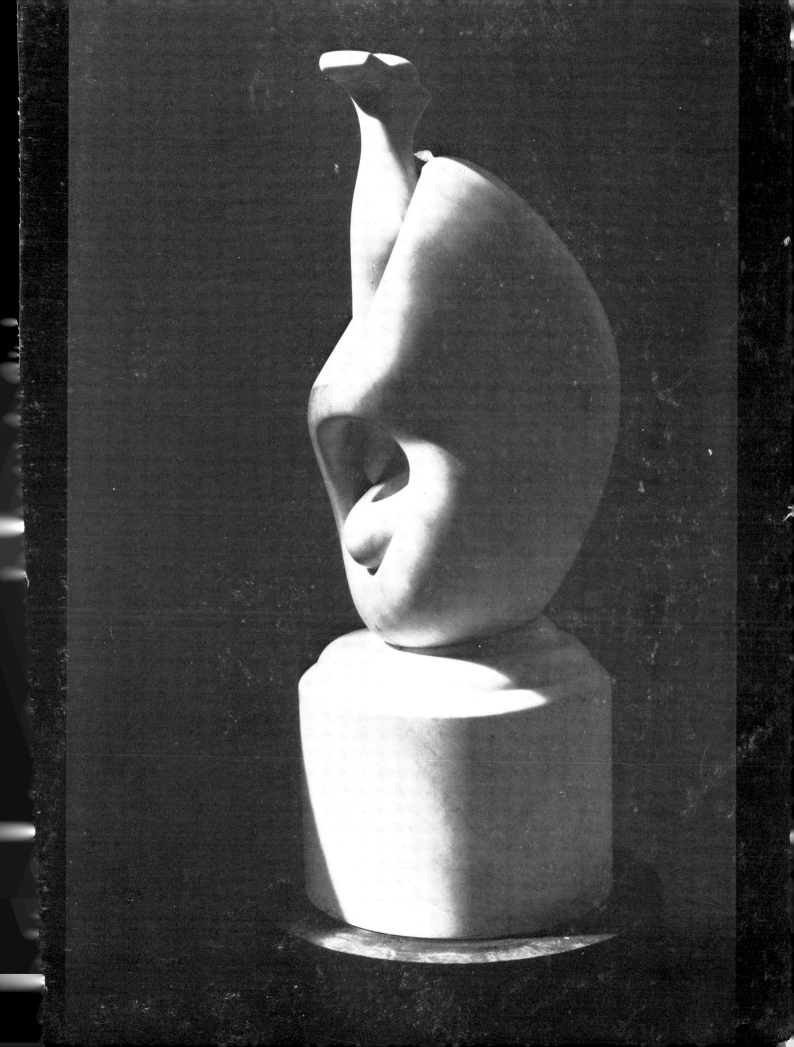

Bronze is a wonderful material, it weathers and lasts in all
climates. One only has to look at the ancient bronzes, for
example, the Marcus Aurelius equestrian statue in Rome. I love
to stand beneath this statue, because it is so big. Under the belly
of the horse, the rain has left marks which emphasize the section
where it has run down over the centuries. This statue is nearly
two thousand years old, yet the bronze is in perfect condition.
Bronze is really more impervious to the weather than most
stone.

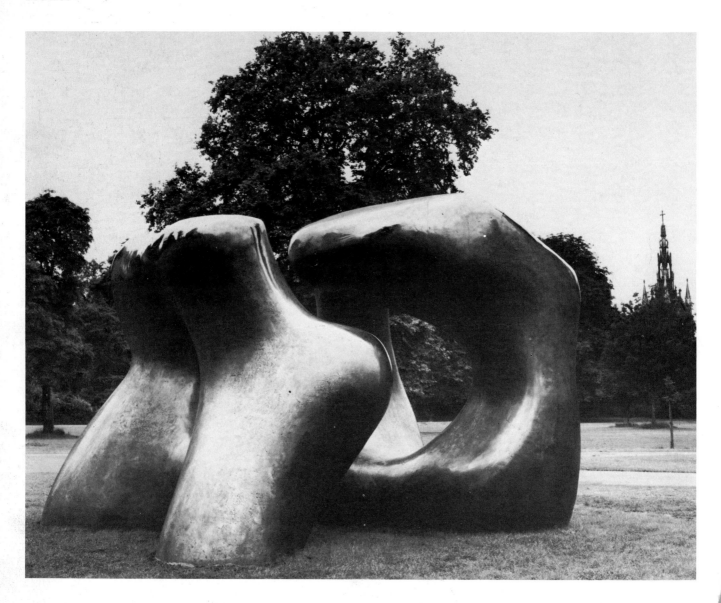

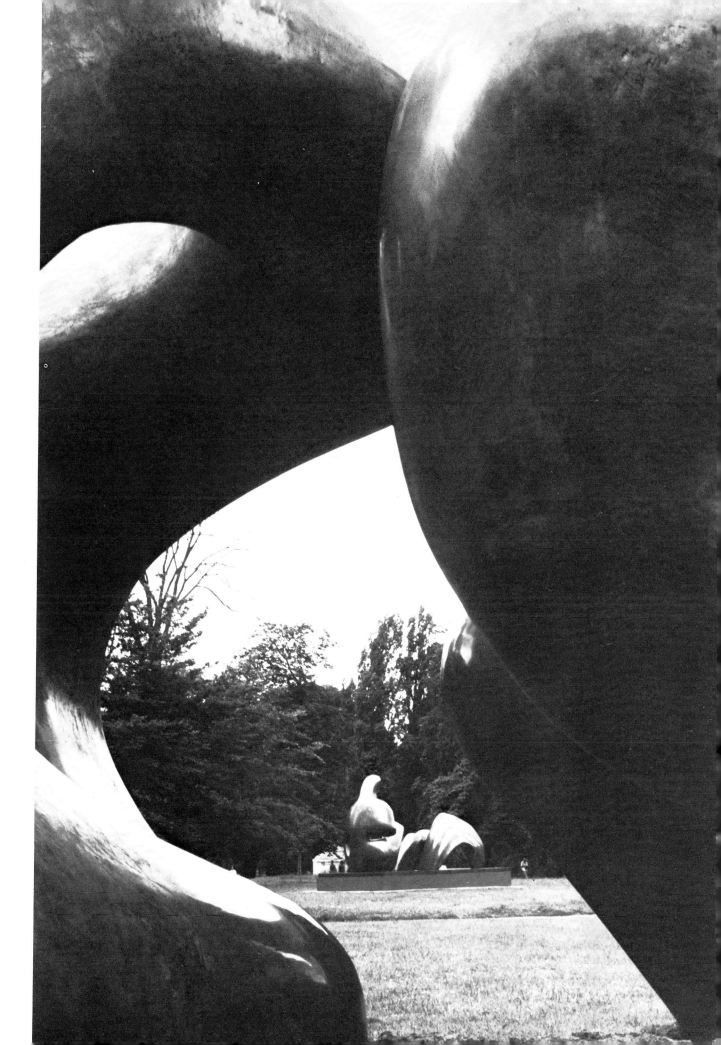

Below and right: *Large Spindle Piece* 1974, in bronze

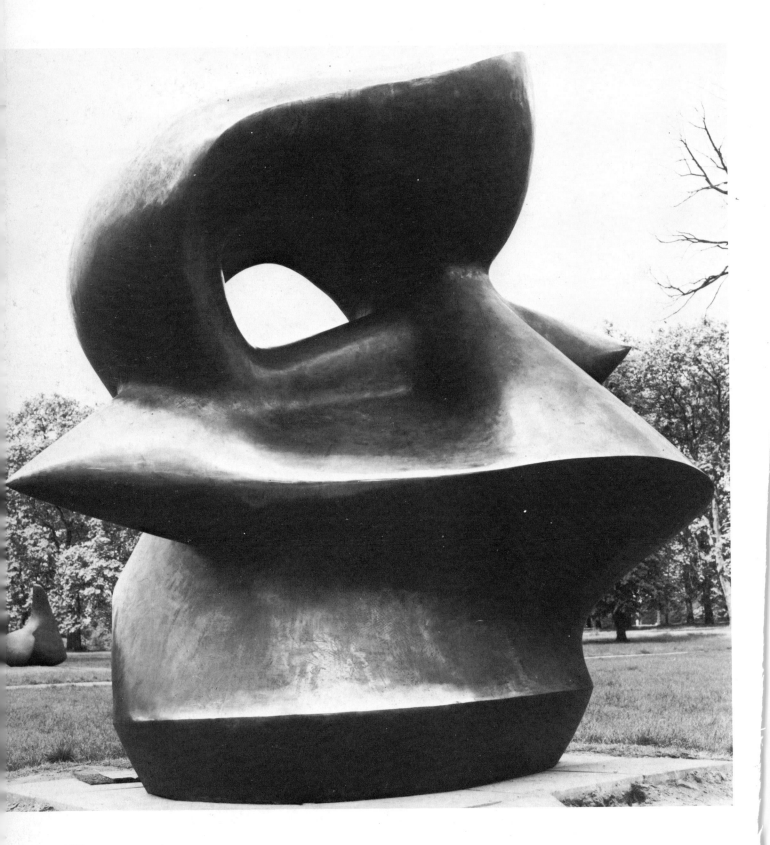

Following pages: *The Arch* 1963/9, in fibreglass, seen across the Serpentine with, in the foreground, *Hill Arches* 1973, in bronze

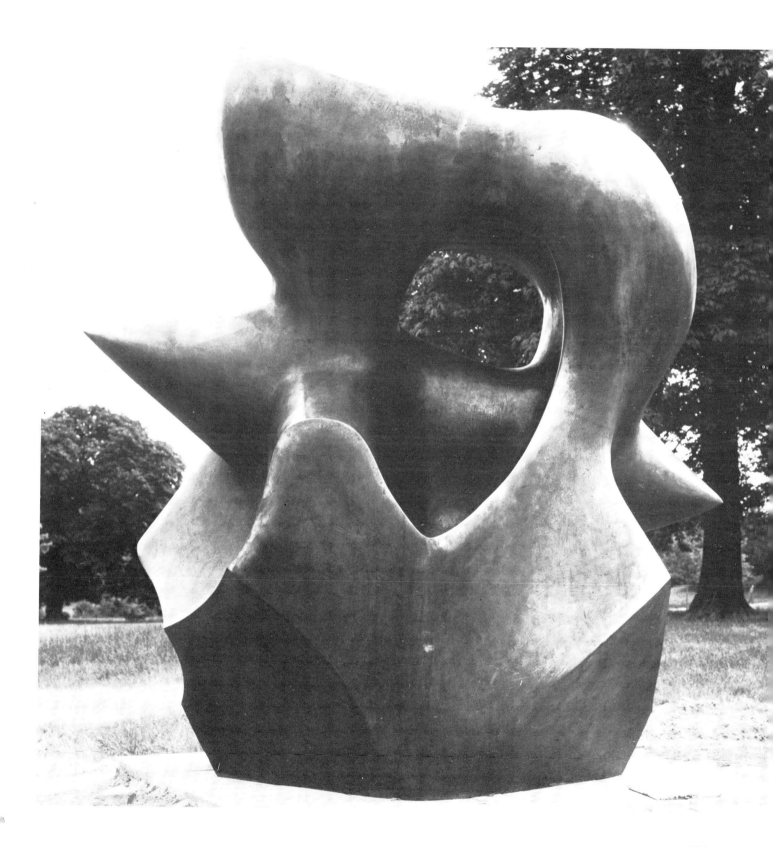

151

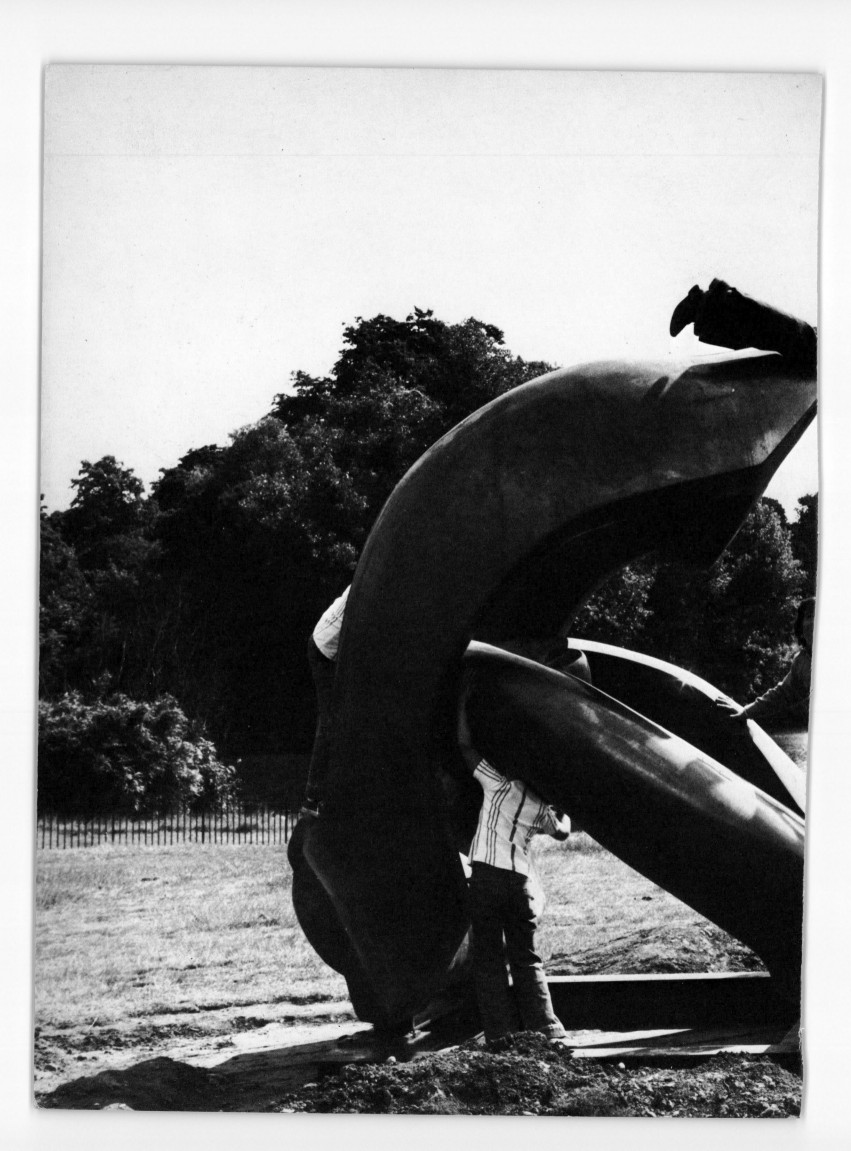

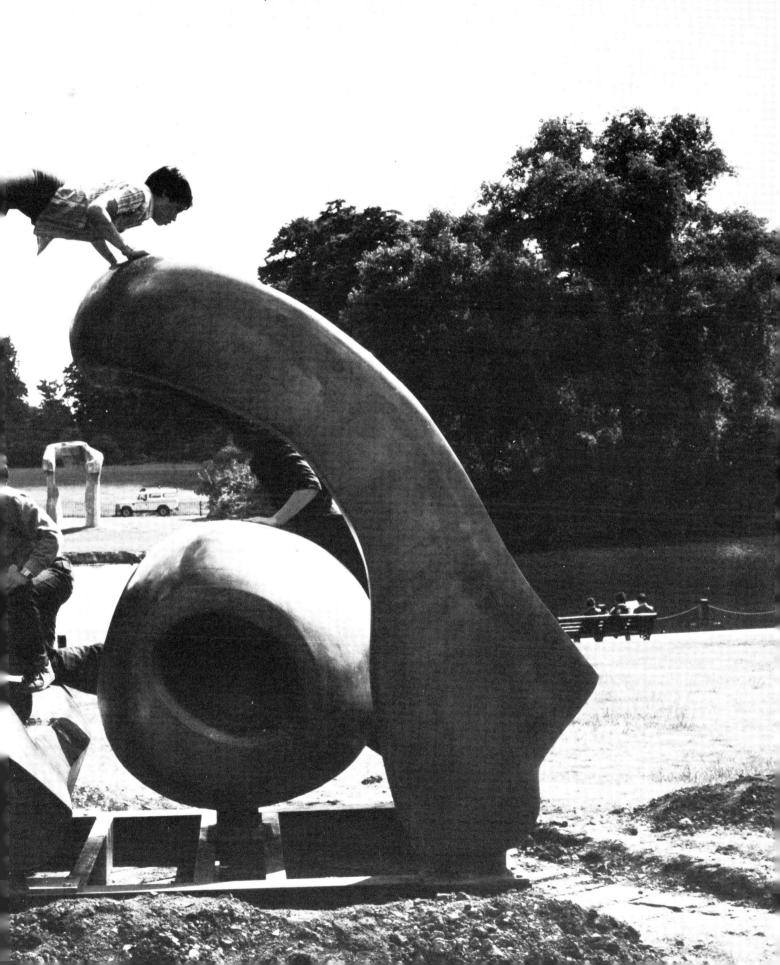

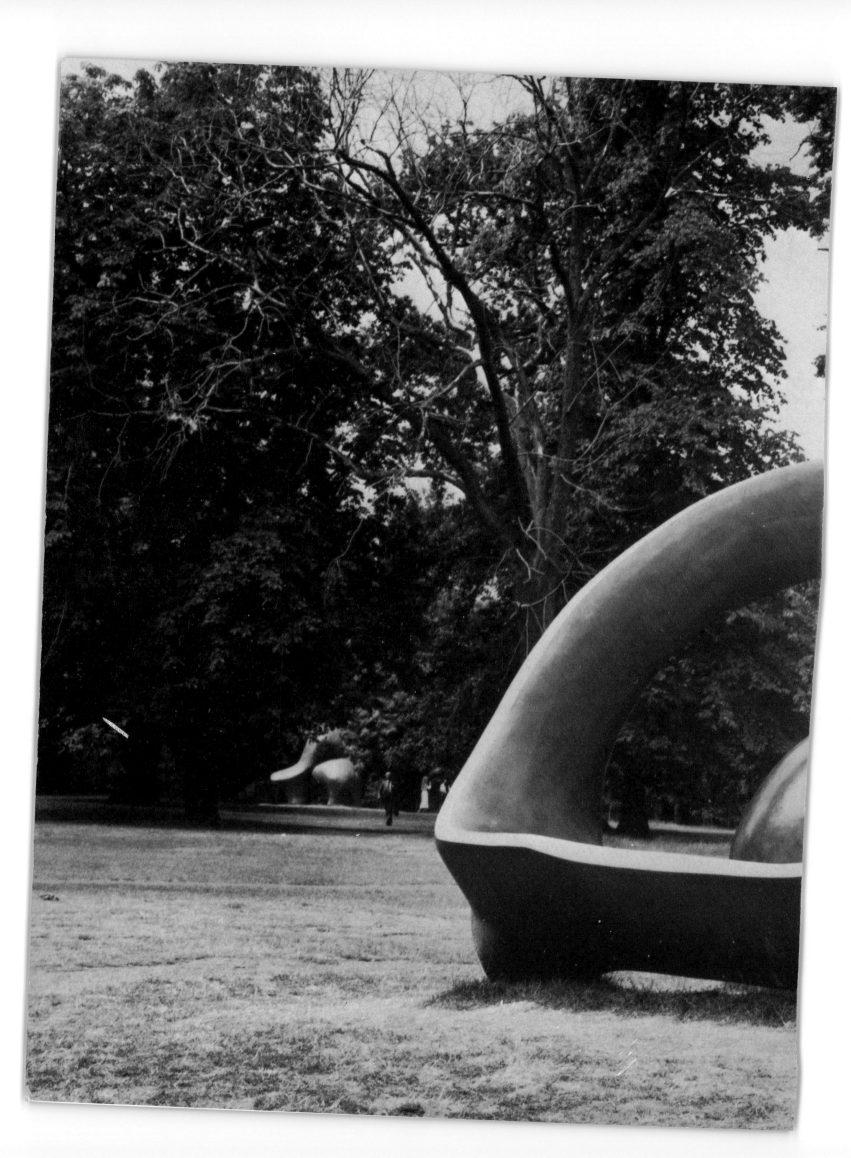

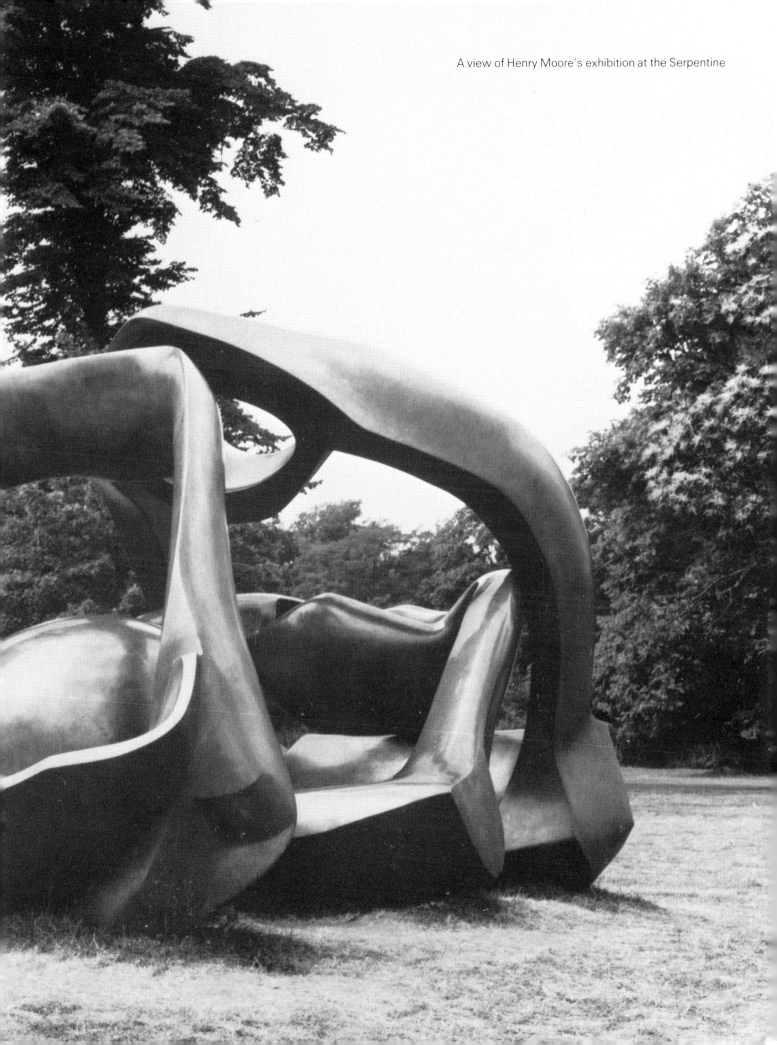
A view of Henry Moore's exhibition at the Serpentine

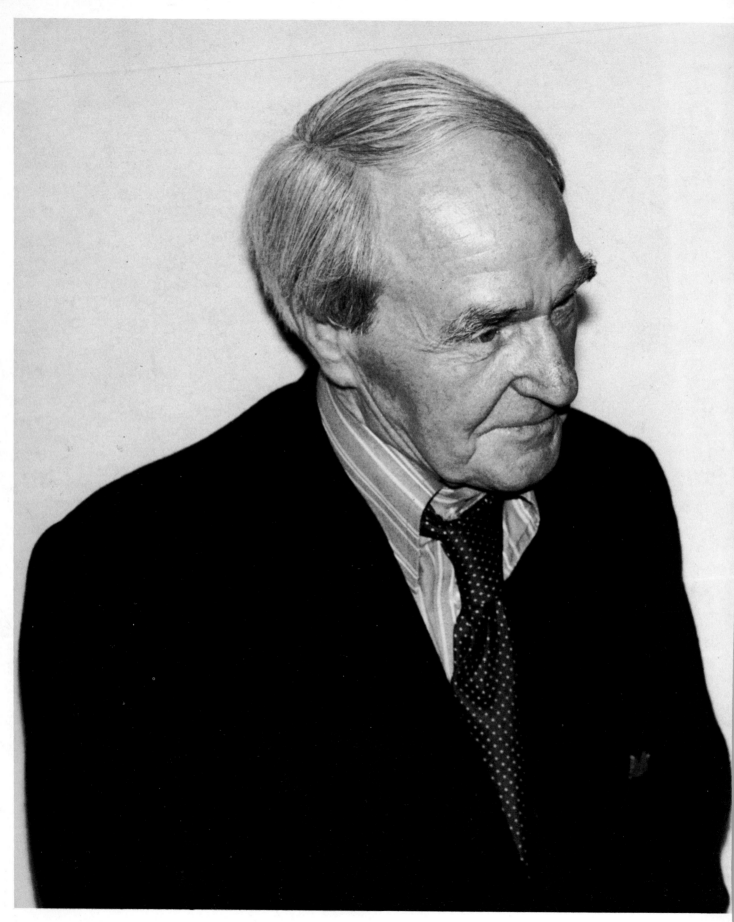

Left: Henry Moore at the opening of his eightieth-birthday Arts
Council exhibition at the Serpentine Gallery, 29 June 1978

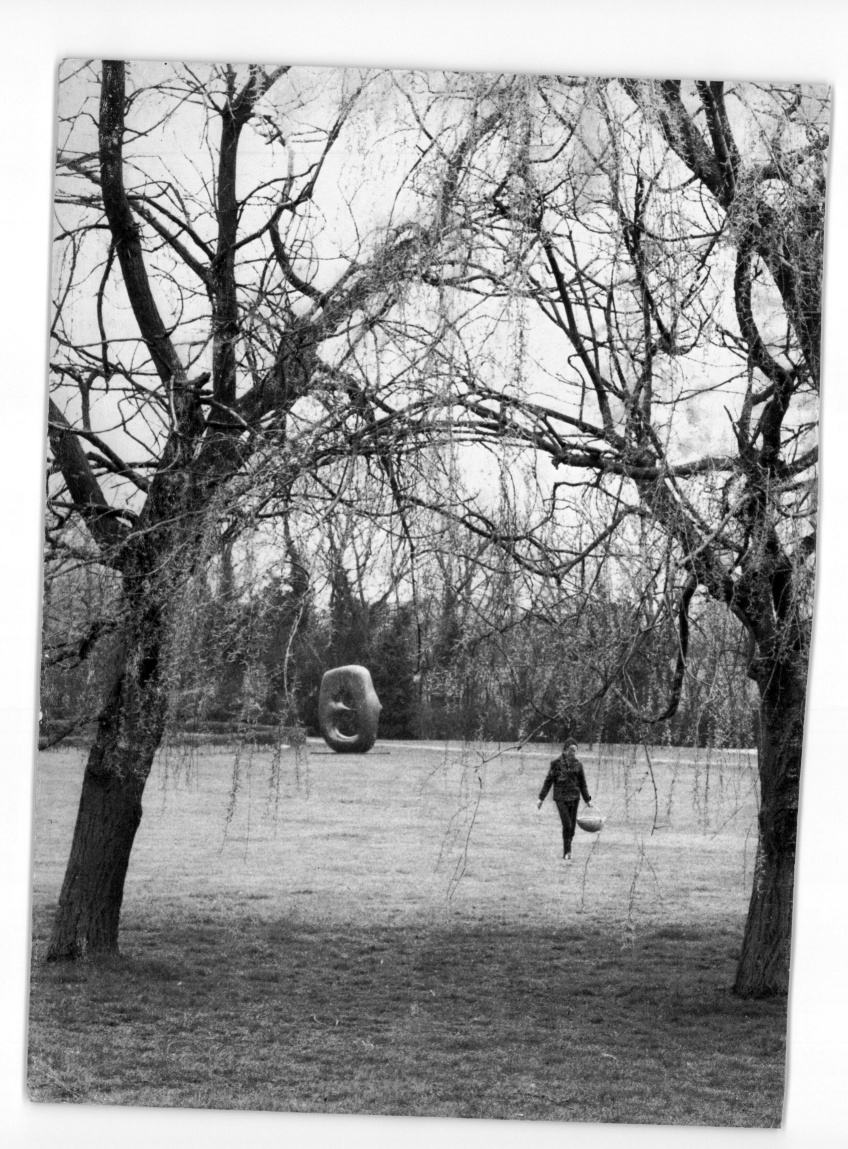